Illustration by Ben Blair

"IT'S A NEWICK"
Legendary designer brought grace and beauty to multihulls.

By Dick Newick and Alison Cotter

Front cover image of Dick Newick courtesy of Jim Brown
Front cover image of Traveller (sailboat) courtesy of Brent Levenson

"IT'S A NEWICK"
Legendary designer brought grace and beauty to multihulls.
Copyright 2015, Pat Newick

Published by BookSpecs Publishing
BookSpecs is a trademark of BookSpecs Publishing, and is registered in the U.S. Patent and Trademark Office.

BookSpecs Publishing, 16 Sunset Ave.,
Pennsville, NJ 08070
http://www.OutRigMedia.com

ISBN 978-0-9903276-7-7

INTRODUCTION

When Tom Follett shocked the sailing world by sailing the diminutive proa 'Cheers' to a third place finish in the 1968 Observer Single Handed race, few people had heard of Dick Newick.

At the time, Jan and I had been successfully building iceboats and class C racing trimarans for some years and were in the beginning stages of forming Gougeon Brothers, Inc.

We were so impressed with the boldness and originality of the 'Cheers' project that I wrote Dick a letter of congratulations. Dick immediately wrote back thanking me and mentioning that he had heard of us and was interested in our approach of using epoxy to bond and seal wood structures. This was the beginning of a lifelong friendship that came to benefit us both in many ways.

As the multihull movement progressed we gained high respect for Dick's philosophy and judgment on the basic parameters of offshore multihull performance. His KISS (Keep it Simple Stupid) principle for racing and cruising was a core belief that ran through all his designs. Dick would regularly send us a copy of his latest design effort for comment. We were always honored that he trusted our judgment and we did our best to earn this trust. In return Dick advised his customers to use our West System Epoxy products and technical support during the build.

Dick stood out from the large pack of multihull designers of the time in one important way: His early experience working with trimarans. Going back to his early days with large offshore multihulls, Dick personally built a series of boats beginning with the catamaran Ay-Ay in 1958, followed by the trimarans Trine and Trice, then putting them to the ultimate test of using them daily in the charter trade. I feel this early experience was the structural key to his future success with 'Cheers' then 'Three Cheers' and others up to 'Moxie,' all of which were built light and strong enough to win races. This gave us great confidence in working with Dick.

In 1977 we teamed up with Dick to build 'Rogue Wave,' which was intended to be Phil Weld's boat for the 1980 OSTAR. It turned out to be a great project where we had a rare meeting of the minds between designer and builder. The result was that this 60' trimaran came in at just under 10,000 lbs.—some 50% lighter than her predecessor 'Gulf Streamer,' a fiberglass boat upturned by a rogue wave and lost at sea.

Unfortunately, when 'Rogue Wave' was half built the OSTAR committee suddenly limited overall length to 56' making 'Rogue Wave' ineligible. Not to be denied, Phil Weld immediately commissioned a second OSTAR boat with Walter Green that was built under time pressure to become the race winning boat 'Moxie.' This setback probably turned out for the best: Dick and I speculated that Phil would not have done as well with 'Rogue Wave,' which had accommodations for six. (Six of us raced 'Rogue Wave' to first place in the 1979 St. Martins Trade winds race.) In contrast, Dick designed 'Moxie' as a special-purpose boat with few amenities, that was lighter and had far less sail area. I look at 'Moxie' as one of Dick's finest designs for a single-handed racing boat. She was easily driven and achieved one of the most unbelievable race wins of all time.

In that era, the OSTAR was considered the toughest and most difficult race of all. At age 65, Phil Weld admitted to never being very athletic. To those who sailed with him, he didn't seem to be a natural sailor. Yet Phil not only handily won the 1980 OSTAR, he set a new course record. Remarkably, he was so rested that following his early morning finish he partied for 20 hours. This was in stark contrast to many who finished behind him who looked like zombies for lack of sleep. In his book, "Moxie," Phil tells a detailed story of how he succeeded and gives full credit to Dick for providing him with an incredible boat that was the perfect fit for the oldest man in the race.

Dick Newick's work has had long-term effects on the lives of many people. One is Fred Ball from Michigan's Upper Peninsula. He contacted Dick after the 1980 OSTAR win, requesting a 'Moxie' style boat that he could also sail single-handed like Phil, but on the Great Lakes. Fred wanted to be involved in the build that would take place close to his home. Due to a shortage of experienced builders it took three years to complete, but with lots of Gougeon support Fred Ball's boat launched in spring of 1985. After several years of tuning, Fred began to win both single-handed and crewed races. After many wins and much cruising over the years, Fred is still at it, winning both the Chicago and Port Huron Mackinaw races in 2014.

Few designers can point to such success; Fred Ball a happy client who has been sailing his dream for 30 years.

There has been much speculation in recent years as to how creative minds like a Dick Newick's really develop. Thus, I was delighted to read in the first chapter of Dick's book details of his educational development over his first 28 years. Dick had the courage and sense to chart a far different course than most. Formal education was an important but minor part in comparison to the eclectic learning opportunities that he sought from people he admired and the many places he ventured to. I think this, together with the extensive reading he did his whole life, (he gave me many heads up on books I should read) was the key to his success as the major pioneer in the multihull movement over this past half century. May he rest in peace.

Read on with joy and as Dick would say, "*Cheers.*"

-- Meade Gougeon

Contents

Foreword... 11

PART ONE

Beginning 16
Family History... 17
The Early Years... 20
Grant's Pass, Oregon... 23
The Navy Years... 25
University of California, Berkley... 27
Now I'm Gonna Build Boats.. 28
Volunteering in Mexico.. 30
Cruising in Europe... 36
Kayaking in Denmark... 38
Winter in a Canadian Minesweeper..................................... 40
Cruising Europe... 41

PART TWO

Moving to St. Croix.. 48
Building the Ay Ay... 50
Meeting Pat.. 52
Starting Charter Business... 56
Trine and Trice are Built with Partner Charles Case..... 59
Preaching Multihulls.. 63
The Charter Crew.. 65
The First Racers.. 68
Tom Follet.. 71
The First Pure Racer.. 74
Cheers: The Retirement Years.. 79

The Racing Years: Three Cheers.................................... 80
Three Cheers.. 83
Moving to Martha's Vineyard.................................... 88
Gulf Streamer.. 92
Spartan Style.. 95
Design Philosophy.. 96
Rogue Wave.. 100
The Val Series.. 103
The Vals and the 1976 OSTAR................................ 106
Keeping it Simple.. 111
Native and Creative.. 115
Creative.. 116
Moxie.. 118
Phil Weld.. 122
Greed for Speed.. 124
Moxie: The Retirement Years.................................. 125
Ocean Surfer.. 126

PART THREE

Moving to Maine.. 131
Echo.. 135
Bird... 138
The Last Design, 'Vaka Fanaua'.............................. 146
Afterward.. 149
Selected Drawings 159
Comments.. 169
Acknowledgments.. 172
Bibliography.. 174

FOREWORD

This book is based on a series of interviews with Dick Newick by Alison Cotter during the summer and fall of 2008, the year Dick was inducted into the North American Boat Designers Hall of Fame. The interviews were tape recorded, transcribed, and shaped into a story. The story captures Dick's unique voice and sense of humor, using much of his own, eloquent words.

It helps that his mind is razor sharp, giving him the ability at age 83 to recount events of the past with remarkable clarity and detail. An added bonus is that he knows the whereabouts of so many of his boats, as the original owners—and even the subsequent ones—feel compelled to stay in touch. Dick says they call out of the blue to tell him they've just had the ride of their lives and that they just wanted to say, *thanks*.

Dick is a wonderful teller of stories, and there are many to tell. He has rubbed elbows with captains of industry, as well as captains of the high seas—the salty rock stars of multihull racing who risk—and sometimes lose—their lives crossing the Atlantic in boats that offer all the comfort of camping tents, just to prove they could. And, because they could, Dick's designs became news, with much of this text made possible because of the numerous magazine articles that featured them.

Dick has also published articles on his designs, written book reviews, and co-authored the book, Project Cheers with Tom Follett and Jim Morris. Unrelated to boats, he wrote letters to Presidents, congressmen and women, created political bumper stickers, and sent hand-written letters to friends and acquaintances all over the world.

Dick Newick has built a career catering to a very small, unique population of the yachting community. In his words, sailboats are a small percentage of the total number of boat sales. Multihulls account for a small—but growing percentage—of that small number, and fast seagoing multihulls are only a part of that number. If you are holding this book, you are probably among this unique, and passionate last group.

This book is dedicated to you. It contains the life story of a designer, whose portfolio now boasts 140 designs, including those that have placed 1, 2, 3, 4, 5, 7 and 10 in the industry's leading race known in Dick's heyday as the OSTAR, the Observer's Single-Handed Trans-Atlantic Race. Philip Thompson, writing for Multihulls Magazine in 1977, calls races such as the OSTAR the breeding ground for Newick's boats. It was the ultimate test of a new idea. The race was originally named for London's Observer Newspaper, the race's main sponsor and primary source of coverage. It has since changed sponsors and names several times.

In the early years of the OSTAR, Dick met Dr. John Norwood of England, founder of the Amateur Yacht Research Society (AYRS). Dick became a long-time vice-president. An amateur by definition, Dick says, is someone who loves what he does. An amateur learns from the success of those who precede him, in a very informal way—mostly because those who precede him are kind enough to share what they know. The group's mission is to provide a forum for sharing information about sailing with those who love the sport.

To illustrate the spirit of sharing, Dick mentions Olin Stephens, designer of seven America's Cup winners and the world's best-known yacht designer for half a century. Sparkman and Stephens was a big New York City firm, with many designers. In essence, Dick says, his studio served as an unofficial school for emerging yacht designers. Dick and he became friends after meeting in Amsterdam at one of the industry's big equipment shows where both were guest speakers invited to exchange ideas and information.

While his main goal was to advance the state-of-the-art, Dick admits that he may have had a slightly more selfish ulterior motive: "One reason that I used to share my designs is that I had nobody to race against." His generosity, however, came with a price. "I suddenly saw my *non*-secrets being claimed as somebody else's original idea." It was Norwood who encouraged Dick to keep at it. "He told me, *The damn fools are going to copy the wrong thing anyway,* and he was semi-right." Dick joked that some people think that copyright means they have a right to copy.

Today, Dick's contributions are recognized the world over by professionals and amateurs alike. Steve Callahan, writing for American Yacht Review in 1999, said it best: "Few, if any, designers have influenced their field as much as Dick Newick. Since he first began creating trimarans in the early 1960s, Newick has changed the lines, angles, and curves of these multihulls into a new genus of tri."

A compliment paid to Dick was given by Olin Stephens himself. Stephens was giving a talk at the Society of Naval Architects and Marine Engineers. Dick says that there were usually about 25 people in attendance, but this time there was standing room only. Someone in the audience asked, *"Have you ever designed a multihull?"* And, Olin said, *"No, I think Dick Newick does a good job of that and I leave that to him."*

With 100 designs built to his credit, 40 more never built and a few series produced, Dick's boats can be found the world over. Val, named after his second daughter, became an entire class and her name, along with her father's, synonymous with the multihull world.

Each boat, of course, is thoughtfully named by its owner, but that's just what's painted on the hull. Ask any owner what they call their boat, and they'll be happy to tell you, *"It's a Newick."*

-- Alison Cotter

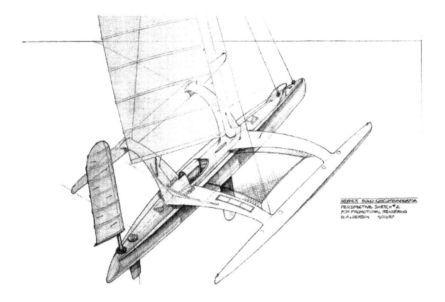

Drawing courtesy of Bruce Alderson (4/20/87)

PART ONE

The 1976 OSTAR was the first race in the sport's history in which multihulls became the dominant competitors. But, as early as 1970, British writer, Jack Knights hints at this possibility.

In a March, 1970 article in Yachts and Yachting that he wrote after a Caribbean inter-island passage with Dick aboard his 36 foot trimaran, *TRICE*, Jack speculates about the future of multihull racing.

> It occurred to me at the time that *TRIAL* went so well, steered so easily, climbed those six foot waves with such agility, not only because she had been well designed and tied together but because she had been kept light. Time and again, multihulls are so over laden that they take undue punishment and become very wet—which leads their crews to reduce sail earlier so that they are soon recording passage speeds no faster than heavy monohulls.

> Haven't we got it all wrong? Multihulls, with their more easily driven hulls, their less expensive construction* and their need for crewing attention are surely meant to be the racers. Heavy displacement monohulls, on the other hand, with their ability to look after themselves, with their great internal volume and carrying capacity are better fitted to be cruisers. Yet because our offshore racing organizations were formed and hardened before the multihull renaissance,

multihulls spend far more time cruising than racing. They don't have the races even if they wanted them. Those keen on racing have not got into the habit of looking towards them.

Not all will agree that trimarans make less than perfect cruisers. Dick Newick, having built himself a wonderful new house overlooking the harbor, has just realized how much money it would fetch if sold. This has made him keen on designing and building a 46-foot tri, then selling out and piling his family aboard for a global girdle.

I know one thing, if I needed a trimaran for any purpose I would first of all consult Dick Newick—if I could find him.

Dick said that is usually not the case.

Family History

Dick Newick has led a fascinating life, one that some might envy. From an early age, the simple phrase "to play with boats" became his driving force. It determined where he lived and how he earned a living, but to understand how someone decides to dedicate his life to playing with boats, one must step back in time to the people who brought Dick into the world and to those who shaped his early experiences.

Evelyn Cooper, Dick's mother, lived in Rutherford, New Jersey where her family had established a considerable reputation.   Her father, William Cooper, moved to Rutherford in the 1890's. Her grandfather served as the city's Mayor and founded the family's successful lumber business.

Born in 1890, Evelyn had a reputation of being an independent woman—unusual at the time. She lived in her parents' home, worked in her father's business, and could even change a tire on his Cadillac. She had an adventurous spirit and didn't marry until what was considered at the time to be late in life.

Naturally, Evelyn was drawn to a man who shared her adventurous spirit: Richard "Rich" Newick. At age 19, Rich went to the Klondike in search of gold. He and a friend went over Dawson's Pass, bought a dugout canoe and a map, and headed down the Yukon River. The pair got lost and traveled for two weeks through an area not even on the map.

Needless to say, Rich never made a nickel in gold mining. He came back to New Jersey where he joined his three brothers in the family business.

Samuel Newick, Rich's father, had opened a steel engraving shop in the New York City Financial District near Wall Street. Tiffany's was one of his clients.   When demand for steel engraving dropped during the Depression, the business moved to Newark and switched to printing, specializing in advertisements and business documents, including some for Thomas Edison. When their father died, the sons took over. *"They were the Newicks of Newark,"* Dick jokes.

Evelyn and Rich married in 1925, when she was 36 and he was 41. The newlyweds took a train to Denver, bought a Model T, and toured the West for three months. This was at a time when there were not very many paved roads.

Camping Honeymoon

Evelyn kept a diary throughout her adult life, and on the honeymoon trip she wrote: "*Stayed at the Grand Canyon today and hiked out to Outer Point in the morning and looked down into some depths. Also climbed the 200 foot look-out tower on a ladder and Rich after me. It took quite a bit of courage for me to get way up to the top where we saw on the rail of the platform, Rich's initials—carved there in 1920 when he was there with his brother Sam!*"

After their travels, they headed back to New Jersey and built a house in Rutherford. But, even after becoming Mrs. Richard Newick and settling into their new home, Evelyn found that she was still a Cooper—at least as far as anyone in Rutherford was concerned. And, so were her offspring. Dick was born on Mother's Day, May 9, 1926.

Brother Bob was born 18 months later, and Art four years after Bob.

By now, Evelyn's brother and brother-in-law were running the family lumberyards, one of which was on the Passaic River, and that meant that Dick, surrounded by a loving family, had easy access to what all aspiring boat builders need: wood and water.

The Early Years

Dick's interest in boat building began, as is true for many of his contemporaries, with a simple kayak. He built his first at age 10, as a summer project with his father, called *"Pop."* Dick remembers that his father was interested in boats and always owned one. During World War I, Pop had wanted to join the Air Force, known then as the Signal Corps, but they didn't take him immediately, so he enlisted in the Navy. He ended up being a Chief Machinist, based in Woods Hole, second in command of a sub-chaser on convoy duty. According to Dick, his father was good with his hands, a jack-of-all-trades. *"Pop used to tell me, if you are anything like me, you'll be happier outside than you will be sitting behind a desk."*

Dick and his father were alike in many ways, but not in physical appearance. Dick was a skinny kid. His dad, on the other hand, was powerfully built. Still, neither was very much into team sports. In high school Dick played tennis, but never as part of the school's team and Rich knew his son needed something besides sports to provide him with a sense of pride and accomplishment. Building a kayak, he figured, was a way to help his eldest child develop some skills and confidence.

Both families, Newicks and Coopers, had summer homes on the water.   Pop's was on the Jersey Shore, a block from Barnegat Bay.

The Cooper family's summer home was the perfect place for a kayak project.   Rockwood, as the Lake Hopatcong waterfront property was called, had an old stone house with a dock and boathouse.   The icehouse had been turned into an extra bedroom, which the family called "*The Chateaux*."   According to Dick, it was a lovely place for a kid to grow up.   His grandparents, William and Ella Cooper, were often there with his mother's three siblings, their spouses, and Dick's cousins.   But, his father wasn't happy just sitting around the dock, so he bought a bunch of materials and the kayak project was born.

Kayaks were not popular at the time.   "*Everybody had a canoe, a row boat, or an outboard; Kayaks were almost a curiosity*."   But, all four—canoe, rowboat, outboard, and kayak—required human power, which was the key to Dick's early education in boat design.   In a 1977 interview with Jim Brown for Sail Magazine Dick says, "*I first learned about boat design from boats that I had to push through the water*."

"*My dad built our three kayaks with me in the way. The next year, we built another. When I was 12, I designed and built two for me and a friend, this time without my father in the way, but I'm sure he helped when asked*."

At age 14, Dick sold drawings for a kayak to a schoolmate for $5, marking his very first sale as a boat designer. He also started experimenting with sails. First, he tried rigging them to his kayaks. *"Of course they were terrible. My mother sewed the sails out of an old bed sheet."* He also modified the rigs of the family sailboats, *"Pop bought us a 9-foot boat, which was under-rigged, so the first thing I did was put a big sail on it."*

With each project, Dick learned the nuances of making his boats go through the water more easily. He learned— as he later wrote for Multihulls Magazine's 20th Anniversary Issue—that *"long, slender-and-light shapes were the best."* This notion would become the hallmark of his multihull design philosophy.

Dick also spent time at a local boat club near his home. *"I would go down there and try to melt into the background and read all their magazines. During the Depression, 25¢ for a magazine was a big deal."* From them he made a mental list of boat design books he'd like to own. Whenever his mother asked what he'd like for a birthday, or holiday, the list immediately came to mind. So, in addition to learning through trial and error by building kayaks with his father and on his own, Dick learned by reading throughout his school years. *The Common Sense of Yacht Design* by L. Francis Herreshoff is one of the classics he enjoyed reading again and again. *"It had a great influence on me and does to this day."*

Grants Pass, Oregon

When Dick was a junior in high school, his family left the comfort of Rutherford. That was 1941 when his father's brothers offered to buy him out of the family printing business and Rich invested in an invention to perfect half tones. He was sure his idea would pay off. "But," Dick said, *"before it got off the ground, Eastman Kodak ended up developing a technology that quickly made my dad's obsolete."*

Rich was ready for a change and headed west—this time in a 1941 Desoto with the entire family in tow. For him, the move was an opportunity to start fresh with more possibilities for the boys beyond Rutherford.

They spent a wonderful summer touring with the idea of finding a place to settle. Dick remembers many national parks and scenic coasts. *"When we saw a boat or historical cemetery, I wanted to stop. My brother Bob wanted to stop at horses, and my brother Art – not sure what he wanted to stop for. But, I do know that there were lots of mandatory stops."*

By the time school was about to start, the Newicks still hadn't settled on a new place, so back to New Jersey they went. The boys started school and Rich headed out on his own to finalize his plan. He purchased a motel—then called an auto court—in Grants Pass, Oregon, by the Rogue River. Dick describes it as a very ramshackle place on a priceless piece of real estate. Rich started remodeling at once.

The family joined him in 1942. Even though Dick had accumulated enough credits in Rutherford to graduate from high school, he enrolled and finished out his senior year. Three months later, his father died of a stroke. Evelyn's brother came out to Oregon, and wanted her and the kids to come back to New Jersey to be near family, but she decided to stay and run the motel herself. Years later Dick would talk about his mother's strength and independence in having made the choice to build a life and business on her own with some help from her three young boys.

Dick was 16 years old and beginning to think about his own career plans, which were a little precarious considering he nearly got himself expelled from high school for rolling a cherry bomb under the principal's desk. *"It shook him up. He was a nice enough guy, but I figured he needed shaking up."*

The incident occurred just one week before graduation, and Dick's mother was called into the office for a talk. And, that's exactly what they did. For two hours, about fishing. Of course, Evelyn had no interest in fishing, but she saw an opportunity. So, thanks to her charm and ability for small talk, Dick was able to graduate on time.

The Navy Years

If Dick didn't excel at small talk, he did excel at drafting. He had taken a course in high school and, combining that idea with his love of boats, Dick decided to study Naval architecture. He joined the Navy in 1943—just before turning 17—with the understanding that they would send him to college for an accelerated program. He spent two semesters at the University of Kansas, before transferring to the University of Michigan to major in Naval Architecture.

Only three schools at the time had naval architecture programs, with the University of Michigan being the easiest to get into, according to Dick. *"But, I flunked out because I didn't understand calculus."* In retrospect, Dick thinks that flunking out was probably a good thing. *"If I had stayed with the program, I would have had a degree, and a commission as Ensign before age 20. I would have known everything, been insufferable, more than I was."*

Instead, he ended up in the Great Lakes for boot camp. After which, he intended to become a machinist. *"I didn't much care for bureaucracy, so I thought I would do best on one of the Navy's smallest ships, a PT boat. And, the only way to get on a PT boat was to learn how to fix diesel engines, so I needed to become a machinist's mate."*

Ranked third in his class of 900 enlisted men, Dick was likely to get his top pick. Not so. Rather than ship him off to machinist school, the Navy decided to ship him out to sea, which offered two possibilities. Either Dick would be assigned to a sea plane tender, or worse, a carrier, which seemed grim, as with the end of World War II still three months away, they were being *'kamikazied'* on a regular basis. While Dick waited for his assignment, a call came in. Pearl Harbor needed a draftsman. It was a temporary assignment, and the caller wanted to know if he would take it. Dick was lucky. When the temporary assignment ended, he was asked to stay. So, he spent his weekdays drawing charts in a hydrographic office in Honolulu and his weekends sailing near Waikiki. Dick said, *"It was an embarrassingly good way to spend the last days of the war."*

When Dick returned to civilian life, his plan was to run the family auto court. His younger brother, Bob was studying art, and Art was in junior high. Their mother, now remarried, had leased out the motel. Dick figured if he came home, ran the business and made money, then he could build boats. His mother, however, didn't agree. She wanted Dick to finish his education, insisted in fact. Dick's parents had not gone to college. Still, both valued education highly. *"My father quit school in the 8th grade. In those days they forced left-handed people to write with their right hand. It was a traumatic experience for my father. He decided he didn't want any more of that, so he quit. Years later, when he had kids of his own, he was very dogmatic about getting an education. It's the only thing they can't take away from you, he said."* So, to honor his mother's wishes, off Dick went on the GI Bill to the University of California at Berkley in 1946.

University of California, Berkley

Dick enjoyed his two years at Berkley where he was active in the sailing club. In fact, he admits to spending more time on the bay—sailing and racing International 14s—than in the library. Yet, he doesn't rank himself among the school's elite sailors, who at the time included Noel North and Bill Ficker, who were already Starboat sailing champions.

Dick and his Oldsmobile

Dick lived in a co-op, similar he says to Berkley's International House, which was sponsored by the Rockefellers. With both the GI Bill and his mother contributing toward expenses, Dick had enough money left over to buy an old wreck of an Oldsmobile. *"It should have been a chick magnet. The problem was that I wasn't a chick magnet. Before we moved West, I was having my* teeth straightened. *That was put on hold during the War and resumed just as I was leaving for college. I didn't have much of a social life and, of course, I blame it on the braces.*"

He graduated in 1948, with a degree in Business Administration, which according to Dick was the easiest one to get. His plan? To go home, hand the diploma to his mother, and say, "*Here, mom, I'm educated. Now I'm gonna build boats.*"

Now I'm Gonna Build Boats

By way of job hunting, Dick put an ad in Rudder Magazine and Yachting Magazine: '*Looking for a job in the boating industry.*' He got one reply. It was for low pay at a small boat shop in Eureka, California. The shop offered plywood, small craft boats, which Dick felt were of mediocre quality, series produced, not custom designed.

Dick moved to Eureka in 1948, and, because of a lackadaisical owner, found that the company was in very bad shape. He was one of three employees.

Instead of taking a full salary, he simply took enough to live on. At the time, Dick thought, "*I'm not going to make money until this place is making money.*" Soon enough, he was pretty much running the place, with the owner off commercial fishing.

It became his first real design job, complete with on-the-job training. His college years had supposedly prepared him to run a business, but he hadn't much design experience. *"I had some of the basic engineering courses during the War but there was an awful lot I didn't know about design and engineering. To this day, I regret that I didn't get the technical education. It would have helped me a great deal over the years."* In the end, Dick says he got a lot of education the hard way: by trial and error. *"Mostly error. We always learn more from our mistakes than from our successes."*

At the same time that Dick was becoming educated about design, he was also becoming more cultured, thanks to a new girlfriend. She was the sister of one of the shop's youngest employees. Her father, Reg White, was a professor at Humbolt State and World War I prison camp survivor. He held a Doctorate in Education from Stanford and was credited with setting up the first indoctrination program at San Quentin prison. *"I got my first taste of a classic education just being around that family. Good music, good art, and fascinating people."* In fact, the White family made such an impression on Dick that he refers to those years as his real education. In particular, Dick remembers that every Thursday, Reg had the college kids come over to read Shakespeare plays together. *"He'd hand out the scripts and give everyone a part."*

Years later, when Reg came to visit Dick and Pat on St. Croix, he remarked how fortunate he considered Dick to be. He said, *"His work and play are the same, and very few people can make that claim."*

Meanwhile, Dick redesigned one of the company's stock boats, resulting in an increase in sales. More sales meant more work, which required more people. Thanks to his Berkley connections, Dick had a ready supply of sailing buddies who were up to the task. By the end of three months, the shop was turning a profit. At this point, the owner resurfaced, expecting to take over management. Dick said he liked the current arrangement just fine, and eventually talked him into leasing him the business.

Dick managed the boat shop until 1952, when the Korean War made materials hard to get. By that time, the owner was off studying how to build boats, so Dick just locked the doors and left.

Volunteering in Mexico

After Dick locked the doors of the Eureka Boat shop, he decided to take some time off. He got in touch with the American Friends Service Committee, a Quaker organization which included people of various faiths who are committed to social justice, peace, and humanitarian service. Dick wasn't a Quaker, but he greatly admired them. He especially appreciated their efforts to make the world a better place through volunteer service projects, which he says the Peace Corp was later patterned after.

Dick wanted to do volunteer work in India. *"I had read most of Gandhi's works, and I was really attracted to what he was trying to do before he was assassinated in 1948."* But the Friends suggested that Dick start off a little bit closer to home. They proposed Mexico, where conditions in some areas were somewhat the same as in India.

Dick joined a summer work camp in the mountains of central Mexico made up mostly of college students. This experience gave him a chance to get acquainted with the Friends organization and their various Mexico projects. He was able to visit several villages, gain valuable insights, and hear about future plans. The project that piqued his interest most was a school being built for the Seri Indians, an isolated tribe on the Sonora Coast.

Their history included Spanish missionaries who believed they were *"civilizing"* the natives along the coasts of Mexico and California, but the Seris revolted. They retreated to Tiburon, an island off the coast of Desemboque, using boats made from reeds that grew along the shore.   Dick says

Seri Country

these were similar to what Egyptians were using thousands of years before. The reed boats would last six months before they became water logged and disintegrated. The Mexicans couldn't follow them because there was no wood in the area to build boats, and the Seris, before departing, had deliberately burned what was left of the reeds.   In 1911, however, the Mexican government sent a gunboat with cavalry to massacre the Indians. One of the survivors still lived in 1953.

Dick met that survivor and learned that the hatred the Seris felt for the Mexicans was still very much alive. The feeling was mutual and exacerbated by the fact that the Seris occasionally stole the Mexican ranchers' cattle, which grazed on what the Seris believed to be their land. When Dick drove his truck into Kino Bay to buy supplies, the Mexican store keepers would hear that he was living with the Seris and ask, "*Where's your gun?*" Dick never felt that he needed one.

Much like the missionaries before them, the Quakers thought it would be a good idea to educate the Seris and get them assimilated, but the Quakers approached the situation in a much more peaceful, less threatening way. Dick agreed to a certain extent, but mostly he was drawn to the project because of its remote, coastal location, a good place for boats.

At the time that Dick lived with them, the Seris were probably the most isolated group of people in North America—sixty-plus miles from a paved road. The Seri Indians were fishermen. They used motorboats, even though they couldn't really afford the motors or fuel, which were given to them by the fish traders. As a result, the Seris were indebted to them for their fuel use. "*Talk about the company store!*" Dick had high hopes for breaking the cycle by luring them—or at least the next generation—back into sailing. Forty-eight years later, he would have a similar mission in southern India.

Dick's kayak "Friend" on pickup

Dick made his way down to Mexico in his 1946 Studebaker pickup truck, sleeping by day, driving by night, and trailing a 14 foot sailboat for the trip. *"Since there were no roads, you had to travel at night in order to steer through the desert by the stars."* Dick was only the third volunteer to be assigned to the Seri project. One of his concerns was the language barrier. *"They were just learning to speak Spanish, as I was. Although I had a year of Spanish in college and two years of French in high school, what came out was Sprench."*

The Seri's had named their first volunteer *"Yosh."* It's an Indian word for the Spanish *"Dios,"* meaning God. Dick added, *"It was given to him because his long, brown beard made him look like Christ from the religious calendar painting that had been left there by the missionaries. The second volunteer also had a long, brown beard and they called him God's brother. Then I came along with a long,*

33

brown beard. They weren't sure that God had that many brothers!"

So, Dick got a new name. He arrived at dawn, tired and very dusty. "I was wearing my mechanic's coveralls, and they'd never seen that. They decided to call me *"Enqui-tames."* Lucky for Dick, a young missionary couple was also stationed there at the time. They were studying the Seri language and actually produced a Seri-English dictionary during their stay. They were able to translate the new name for Dick. Enqui-tames: guy who has to get undressed to take a crap. *"It was always said with a big smile."*

Dick and Tavo, (Octavio Zenil) a Mexican volunteer, were charged with finishing a schoolhouse. A home for the school's new teacher was complete, and the school was well underway. The two volunteers ate their meals with the teacher and his family, a Mexican man who was raised in Los Angeles. Dick and Tavo completed the adobe walls, built windows and doors, made benches and tables, and tarred the flat roof.

Dick and his wife, Pat, returned to Mexico some 30 years later to find the school abandoned, just melting into the ground, and half the tribe living in government housing, a few miles from Desemboque. *"To an outsider, it would look as if our work there had been a complete waste of time, but it wasn't wasted at all for us because we got to know the Seris."*

Dick remembers in particular an Indian woman who saved his life in an incident involving his sailboat which he kept on a beach. *"One of the Seri men took my boat, got blown down the coast and came ashore."* Dick ran down to meet him, but before he did he asked the other men of the tribe if that person would have taken one of their boats without permission. They said no. So, when Dick met up with him on the beach, he was angry and used his limited Spanish to say so. *"I said, you're a no good girl who can only steal and can't sail, and that made him really mad."* When Dick turned to continue walking toward his boat, the Seri picked up a huge rock, intending to brain me with it. The teacher was watching from the roof and saw one of the girls grab his arm. *"She wouldn't let him throw it."*

That girl, Maria Baylin, was still there 40 years later, when Dick and Pat returned to visit. She was now an old woman, sitting in the shade of her little house, making jewelry to sell to the tourists. *I said, 'Hello,' and she grunted.*

'I'm Dick Newick, Do you remember me?' No she didn't. *I said, 'I'm Enqui-tames.'"* Her eyes lit up. She reached up and grabbed Dick's hands, which Pat later described as the most emotional moment of their visit. Maria Baylin went into her house to pick out two shell necklaces to give to Dick and Pat. In return they gave her a colorful blouse and

a jar of honey. She hid the gifts under her shirt to keep from sharing with the rest of the tribe.

In the end, Dick says, *"I'm not sure we did them any favors, they were nomadic people, fishermen and hunters, we settled them down with our school, but it might not have been a good thing."* And, Dick never did charm the Seri's into giving up their motorboats for sailboats. Sailing was a hard sell; the motorboats were so much faster. Some days, after he finished his work, he spent time on the beach building kayaks to show the Seris new construction techniques. And every chance he got, he'd take the kids out sailing in the beautiful Gulf of California. *"When Pat and I drove over the last hill, she took in the amazing view of the Gulf and said, 'Now I understand what this place means to you.'"*

Cruising in Europe

When Dick and his fellow volunteer and new friend, Tavo, returned to the states, they headed to San Francisco. Dick helped Tavo find work with a Quaker family, and Dick found a job with a local boat builder. It was 1953 and Dick was 27 years old.

Dick viewed the job as a stepping stone. His spare time was spent building a kayak that he planned to take to Europe. By the summer of 1954, after what Dick supposes was about six months on the job, he had saved enough to finance the trip. *"I put the boat on the top of the pick up and went to New York to find a way to get to Europe."* But first, Dick took a quick side trip to Marblehead, Massachusetts, to the home of L. Francis Herreshoff.

L. Francis Herreshoff was the son of legendary yacht designer Nathanael Herreshoff, who revolutionized yacht design and produced a number of America's Cup winning yachts between 1893 and 1920, which is now known as the Herreshoff Period. *"He designed and built more boats than anybody for the America's Cup races, until Olin Stephens came along."* L. Francis was a famous designer in his own right and also the author of numerous books on yacht design, which Dick had read and reread since childhood. *"His books influenced me more than anything else. L. Francis had a kayak; I arrived with my kayak on my way to Europe. I wanted to show him mine and see his. Of course, his was better."*

Still, Dick got a nice welcome and was invited up to Herreshoff's studio, located on the top floor overlooking the harbor. There was a drawing board—maybe 30 feet long—where L. Francis could spread everything out; also a lathe and small milling machine for making his own hardware and trying out new ideas. *"There was a group there, so I just hung around the periphery of the conversation."*

Herreshoff was a bachelor and very cordial, according to Dick. *"A real iconoclast, which you wouldn't expect from the son of the most famous designer that ever lived. A lot of what he wrote was just classic."*

After that, Dick would correspond occasionally with Herreshoff (their letters are part of the Maritime

Museum's archives) and stopped in to see him every time he came through Marblehead. One memorable time Herreshoff offered to take Dick to the grocery store to stock up on supplies for a trip to St. Croix. They drove in his Italian sports car. *"It was either a Lamborghini or a Ferrari and we never went more than 25 miles per hour."*

Kayaking in Denmark

Dick found a freighter that was taking 12 passengers to Europe for $200 apiece. Moreover, they were willing to take his boat. *"Sure, throw it onto the deck."* And, so he crossed the Atlantic and, as Dick puts it, happened to land in Antwerp.

"When we arrived, they lowered my kayak into the water. Somebody pointed me in the direction of the canal, and off I went." That's when Dick got a little nervous. He had no idea what was going to happen next. His French was terrible. He spoke no Flemish at all. And, the

waterways were made up of a complicated system of locks, each controlled by a lock keeper, who probably spoke only French or Flemish. As Dick approached the first lock, he breathed a huge sigh of relief. *"The keeper was reading the Saturday Evening Post. He introduced me to a skipper of a 180-ton tanker who was entering the lock. I ended up traveling aboard the tanker for two days with the crew of two. Neither one spoke much English. But, the captain's wife was having their first baby so the stateroom was free. So, here I was in my own varnished mahogany stateroom, headed for Copenhagen."*

The two months he spent traveling the rivers and canals of Holland and Germany were much less luxurious in comparison to his stateroom stay. The summer of 1954 was a wet one with only six days without rain. Dick didn't have a tent when he started the journey, but quickly purchased one. He spent his days paddling or sailing and sometimes catching a ride or a tow. At night, he slept in haystacks or under bridges or in farmers' lofts. Occasionally, when the weather was really bad, he'd sleep in a pension or youth hostel. Dick estimates that he traveled 1,000 kilometers in those two months, letting his ears plot the course: *"Every time I heard an American accent, I'd go the other way."*

Winter in a Canadian Minesweeper

After two months navigating the canals, Dick was ready for open water. He bought an 18-ft Utzon-designed lapstrake double-ender named *Amiga* in Denmark for $575 from a boat builder who agreed to store the kayak (Friend), which is now on display at the Maritime Museum in Newport News, Virginia. He spent another two months exploring Denmark and meeting new people, but winter was coming and Dick needed a place to stay, a cheap place. Through his many contacts, Dick was put in touch with Ulle Christiansen, a Dane who wanted to learn English, and a trade was established. He would share his place with Dick in exchange for teaching him. *"When I first met Ulle, he thought he was speaking English and I thought he was speaking Danish!"*

He was a 50 year old recluse who sailed a superb 23-foot oak planked Colin Archer type sloop. He refused to pay taxes for what he called war or socialism. And, the best way to get out of paying taxes, he decided, was to not earn anything. His home was an abandoned Canadian minesweeper. According to a May 2005 interview with Dick for Latitude 38,

Ulle Christiensen and his beautiful Colin Archer

"The minesweeper was being converted to a fishing boat and was getting a completely new bridge, so this fellow bought the old bridge, plopped it down on a plot of land on the waterfront and lived in it." In the interview, Dick is quoted as saying, *"We had no electricity, and the only heat we got was from breaking up a series of derelict boats for firewood. You can learn a lot about boat construction with a sledgehammer and an axe. It was easy to see what worked and what didn't."*

During the time that Dick spent on the bridge with his Danish host, he discovered a means of making some extra money: Folkboats. San Francisco sailors loved them. Dick spent part of the winter hitchhiking around the country buying Folkboats and shipping them back to Jack McNickles who sold them in San Francisco. According to the Latitude 38 story, *"At least part of the class's enduring popularity can be traced to a budding, young, yet-to-be multihull designer."* They were solid 25-foot boats with big iron keels that would have cost three times as much to build in the United States.

Cruising Europe

"After the War, Europe was depressed, and the dollar was king. I was living on top of the wave, with dollars in my pocket. Economics were on my side." The money Dick made allowed him to devote all of 1955 to cruising. He shipped his kayak, *Friend,* back to Jack in San Francisco and found passage aboard a 62-foot ketch *Santa Maria,* built in 1907. The captain Asker Kure planned a world

cruise. Dick signed on for the leg to San Francisco. *"If we get that far!"* joked the captain.

Dick describes Asker as a smart, very articulate guy, who spoke nearly perfect English. *"When I later became engaged, I wrote to tell him about the girl of pure Norwegian descent. He wrote back that he was glad to hear that I had chosen a Scandinavian girl, saying, 'You know how I feel about Nordic superiority, not necessarily in intellect but in honesty and steadfastness of purpose.' Those were his exact words, which I read to Pat, and translated for her that Asker was too polite to say what he really meant: she may not be very bright, but she sure as hell is gonna be stubborn!"*

Asker was an old salt. He had spent many years of his youth on American merchant ships. When he got back to Denmark, he bought an old Scottish steam trawler with the money he had saved. It was probably built in the 20's, about 100 feet long, had the shape of a sailing vessel. He re-rigged it as a sailing vessel and delivered cargo all over Europe in the early 1930s. Dick says he was a hard task-master. *"To minimize expenses, he'd get a bunch of kids as crew, feed them potatoes, and whatever fish they could catch."* He also learned the ropes. *"He knew where the smugglers were, how fishermen were using the government to beat the system."* His cargo vessel had been the flagship of the underground Danish Navy, smuggling Jews out of Denmark to Sweden during the war. He still carried a Husqavarna submachine gun with 500 rounds of ammunition, which, for fear of being searched, he and Dick had to toss overboard before entering the Mediterranean during the time of the Algerian uprising.

"One of my regrets in life is that we didn't just throw a tin can in the water and blast away at it. I never got to try that beautiful piece of machinery."

Dick paid him $2 a day for food during their time together. *"He made money on me."* The captain had a weak heart and couldn't exert himself at all. So, the arrangement was that Dick looked after the sails and anchor, while the captain looked after the engine room and navigation. *"We always knew right where we were."*

Santa Maria's bottom was covered with sheets of copper, the best anti-fouling. They docked at Ile d'Yeu to check the un-coppered oak rudder shaft for worms. Dick said, *"We didn't know if she was going to get us around the world or not, so we decided to dry the boat out next to a pier at low tide to get a good look at the hull."*

Santa Maria

"I was very uneasy because the boat had a deep keel, and Asker wasn't used to drying out this type of vessel.
I suggested we take an anchor and put it on the other side of the key, hoisted on the main halyard, which would go up and down with the tide and would give us a heel into the key, so we wouldn't

fall away from it, which would be a disaster." Disaster did strike when the boat fell over in about a foot of tide. *"The anchor came whistling over my head, a sickening feeling, no warning."*

"We tacked canvas onto the worst hole. The local fire department helped with their big pumps. When the tide came in, the boat righted. We spent all of our high tide pumping with the ship's pump and low tide caulking and repairing. It was touch and go, but we got the old vessel so that she was semi-seaworthy." After a short, trial sail to LaRochelle, Asker and especially Dick, sadly said good-bye to Elsa, a Danish woman who had joined Santa Maria for part of the voyage, and now headed back to her home in Paris.

Dick and Asker sailed on down the coast and realized the trip around the world was off. In Malaga they met a German couple, who were traveling by bicycle on a honeymoon, except that Dick later learned they had never actually bothered to get married. He was an engineer. She had a PhD in art history. The couple split up when he returned to Germany and Sigrid stayed on until she and Dick hitchhiked to Paris, stopping at all the historic places along the way. Dick enjoyed touring museums with her after his old flame, Elsa, had left. But, *"having two girlfriends in Paris who knew about each other was not the best arrangement."*

Dick headed back to Malaga, where he had arranged to sail aboard a 40-foot sloop *Adara*, being delivered to the United States. The skipper turned out to not be much of a seaman. The other crew member didn't know how to sail at all. The four made it as far as Barbados, before they parted ways. *"We would have parted sooner, but we were in the middle of the Atlantic and there was no place to go."*

From Barbados Dick found passage on the 90-foot cargo schooner *Arcadius* headed for St. Kitts by way of St. Lucia with general cargo. *Arcadius* suffered a spar mishap, anchored in Castries, St. Lucia. So Dick headed to St. Thomas to make some money. He found passage aboard the 34-foot ketch *Sunrise*, captained by an Austrian, Joe Pachernag. Joe had been an underwater specialist in Hitler's Navy, enlisted in the French Foreign Legion when the war was over, and made a rare escape by jumping ship and joining the Swedish merchant marines. The pair arrived in St. Croix, U.S. Virgin Islands on February 29, 1956 and were urged to stay by hotel owner Jim Hurd, who told them not to bother going to St. Thomas. Too much competition. He said, *"Stay here and I'll keep you busy with charters."* It was the first time Dick had set foot on American soil in 20 months. He had visited a hundred and one ports in eleven countries—all for less than $2,000.

Joe and Dick enjoyed the winter in St. Croix. At the end of the season, Sunrise sailed west and Dick flew to Antigua where he joined Tom Follett and his 23-foot sloop, *Native Dancer*. He sailed with Tom and his friend Bob Wright to Florida. Joe Pachernag later lost Sunrise in the Galapagos, and Dick lost touch with Joe.

Rudder magazine published a series of four articles that Dick wrote about his experiences kayaking and cruising in Europe. The first, "Water Wandering in the Low Countries," appeared in Rudder's September, 1956 issue.

Two others, "Water Wandering in Denmark" and "Water Wandering the Coast of Europe", were in the October and November issues. The last, "Water Wandering the Caribbean" was printed in the January 1957 magazine. An excerpt from the first issue about navigating his 18-foot kayak, *"Friend,"* through the canals and rivers of Germany into Belgium reads:

> The following morning was spent patching the Friend's bow and stern which had been insufficiently reinforced when I built her. While waiting for the plastic to set up, thoughts turned to an improved boat and I decided that for a similar trip, I would prefer a kayak with thirty inch beam and watertight bulkheads for flotation. Also, I would carry far less gear and try to reduce Friend's fully loaded weight from 220 to 150 pounds. A small sail adds greatly to the fun, but complicates the question of beam. This might be solved by a narrow waterline beam with reserve buoyancy for sailing near the sheer.
>
> When the plastic cured sufficiently I took advantage of a gusty favorable wind with rain squalls and made good time. That night was spent under another bridge where I awoke damp and firmly resolved to get a tent and soon my spirits rose as I quickly resumed sailing, shooting off ahead of a tug with five barges. Then they slowly passed me, a tight squeeze in the narrow canal with vessels also passing in the opposite direction. I decided to raise full sail and live dangerously. It was wonderful. The tug and barges were quickly passed and never

seen again. At first I reefed down for the worst squalls, but finally got used to sailing through everything including some very wet downpours and a vicious hail squall. The only regrets were the lack of a watch to time the speed and the lack of a cameraman ashore to record the Friend's performance. I was proud of her.

PART TWO

Moving to St. Croix

The years 1956 and 1957 included many milestones for Dick. During that time, he published his first articles in a trade magazine, launched his first catamaran, and met his bride-to-be. After landing in Florida, he returned to New Jersey to visit his family. While there, he wrote the four Rudder articles. These were the first of many he would publish throughout his lifetime. Dick shared his philosophy on sailing and boat design. Over the years, he gained a wide readership and established himself as an industry innovator.

During the previous winter in St. Croix, Dick decided to build his first catamaran for the day charter business. He liked the place, thought he could earn a living there, and had made some good friends. *"I saw an opportunity in St. Croix to take paying guests sailing."* But, in Dick's mind, the boats currently used in this service were completely unsuited. He thought back to Florida, where he had taken a ride on a 60-foot catamaran, skippered by a man in the charter business. *"I liked the boat and the life he had built for himself."* At the time, there were very few catamarans, especially ones that were designed and built by the owners. Dick saw an opportunity to build not just a life, but also a reputation. His vision required a leap of faith and some capital.

While visiting family in New Jersey, he sold his truck, shipped his tools, and returned to St. Croix in late 1956 to settle down—with what remained of his $10,000.00 inheritance from his father's death. It had been sitting in the bank, virtually untouched. Dick used some to finance his travels, especially when his savings from work or Folkboat profits ran low. But, he had never wanted to use this gift for minor things. He had planned to use the money for something that would make a difference. That something was his first catamaran, the 40' *Ay Ay*.

"I wanted to do a longer boat, but the ones I had designed and built up to that point in my life were 20-feet or under." *Ay Ay* would be twice that. Dick started sketching his first catamaran while in New Jersey and even made another trip to visit his idol L. Francis Herreshoff in Marblehead for suggestions.

In an article on Bird for *American Yacht Review* published in 1999, writer Steve Callahan recalled the early catamarans of the Nat Herreshoff era and their Spartan style, which so many of Dick's designs emulate:

> Nat Herreshoff built several catamarans in the 1890s and thought they would make good cruising boats if kept light enough, though that would require a Spartan, almost camping style of cruising. In fact, when Herreshoff's cats proved so fast the regatta committee had to search for a reason to ban them from racing, they asked Herreshoff if he had any accommodations, which were required. Herreshoff replied, *"Why, yes—a camp stool."* Newick has always carried Herreshoff's torch, if not his stool,

refusing to bloat a multihull's wide platform with penthouses and living rooms. He's always provided the essentials—good sea berths and places to sit, cook, and navigate comfortably and efficiently—but the quarters in his most Spartan racers, often described, including by Green (owner of Bird) as 'coffins,' have led many to consider a *'Newick accommodation'* an oxymoron."

Building the Ay Ay

St. Croix consisted of two main townships, Frederiksted and Christiansted, both named for Danish kings. Dick rented a warehouse about 100 feet from the beach in Frederiksted as his boatbuilding workshop. The warehouse belonged to a quasi government organization and was once used in the sugar cane industry. The workers would make sugar; they also made rum. Dick said, *"St. Croix, in those days, if you were white and had $10 in your pocket, the world was yours. If you had any skill at all and weren't a drunk, you could be successful. Of course, a number of people drank too much because rum was 89 cents a bottle."*

Dick remembers that few Cruzans (St. Croix natives) would work cutting sugar cane, so the government would import workers for every harvest. The labor came from Antigua and other English islands. *"Big, old schooners would pull into the harbor and 150 guys would walk off. Most of them would go home when the work had ended, but some would stay and try to get other jobs. The island was full of illegal workers."* Dick says that he got residency

50

green cards for about ten men who worked at his boat shop and charter business.

In the earlier years, though, Dick couldn't afford to hire workers. He had helpers. *"I had a high school kid and a friend of Pat's as helpers. But, 85% of that boat (Ay-Ay) I built on my own."* It took a full year of long hours, with work stopping periodically when he ran out of money and had to take a job for a few weeks. When *Ay-Ay* was finally finished in the spring of 1957, two of Dick's cousins came down and helped christen the boat—each smashed a bottle of rum on one of the two hulls.

Ay Ay

During that year the warehouse was not just his workshop it was his home. The warehouse had an old concrete floor that had been saturated with molasses, so the place was absolutely full of cockroaches. *"I had my cot with a mosquito net, and I put each leg in a dish of water to keep cockroaches off. I usually ate just one meal a day; two cans of Campbell's soup, undiluted, mixed together. I could make various concoctions out of cream of mushroom and whatever else was around. I usually had some fruit from the local market. Very simple."*

Dick ate better in the offseason when he was offered a bed and one meal a day at Sprat Hall, in exchange for helping out around the place. *"Usually that meant driving the cooks home after dinner, but sometimes that meant scurrying around the old building, putting up storm shutters, during hurricane warnings."* He also had many new friends around the island and often had a meal with them.

Meeting Pat

One morning in August 1957, Dick drove his Vespa motor scooter down the island's one straight road, between the sugar cane fields and there was Pat who had just arrived on St. Croix that very day. She was in her junior year at Hamline University, but decided to take some time off to travel. While the assistant matron of a Lutheran Children's Home in Frederiksted was on leave, Pat Moe had been hired to take her place. A high school friend, Sue Hargraves invited Dick to come to a dinner that night where other friends were coming to meet Pat. Sometime during that first evening, she later told Dick that it just popped into her head that he was the guy she was going to marry. He enjoyed telling people that she must have been desperate that she would end up marrying the first guy she met.

Dick and Pat started spending all of their spare time together, sailing, dinners and dancing on weekends at the favorite, local hang-outs, St. Croix by the Sea, Morning Star, and The Stone Balloon.

When Pat's job as assistant matron ended she worked with John Yntema at Merwin's Shipping Company until she and Dick set a wedding date for May 9, 1958. Jim and Joy Hurd offered their beautiful plantation hotel, Sprat Hall, for the wedding. Dick wore a white jacket. Pat looked stunning in her white wedding dress. A steel band played and about fifty of the couple's island friends danced the night away. *"It was a great party, Dick laughed. The only problem was that we didn't want to leave."*

Fritz Henle, a world-renowned photographer and friend, took all of the photos, and later of Dick's boats, many of which appear in this book.

Ed Karkow offered the newlyweds the use of his 30-foot yawl designed by a famous German firm, Abeking and Rasmussen. They planned to sail 100-miles for their honeymoon, but foul weather conspired against them. Instead, they made it as far as Tortola Harbor and took shelter in a charming, small hotel, Fort Burt, overlooking Roadtown.

Ed had offered and Dick had accepted, a job helping to run a 200-ton marine railway and small hotel that Ed leased on Beef Island, separated from Tortola by a narrow channel. In those days a jeep drove, and passengers stepped onto, a wooden, heavy raft and pulled rope lines to navigate across. A dirt road led the short distance to Trellis Bay where the marina and hotel were located.

Originally, Dick intended to start his charter business, but the skipper he had lined up backed out. So he tied *Ay Ay* up at the hotel and started his new job. *"In those days you could go all day and never see another yacht, now it's full of boats and full of resorts. Rockefeller built a resort five miles from where we were. That resort still has one of my trimarans."*

Pat helped with guests and supplies at the hotel, while Dick worked at the marina. It was the only marine railway that could take care of vessels up to 200 tons between Puerto Rico and Martinique. *"We had most of the yachts and a good proportion of the commercial vessels."*

Dick and Pat's simple cottage was on the beach along with four unfinished others. There was no water, no plumbing, and no electricity. *"We put a 55-gallon drum on scaffolding and one of the help would come every day to fill it with water. The sun would heat it. Pat and I would take turns turning an outside crank to have enough water for a shower. We had a small generator, a kerosene refrigerator. Sometimes they worked, sometimes not. When they didn't, we used kerosene lamps for reading lights."*

Ed's parents came down from Chicago to visit. His father told us, *"You know what you guys are? You're maintenance men. You can't do any management because you are just running around putting out fires."*

Not long after, Ed sold his lease, married Kirsty Parker, (they became lifelong Newick friends,) and moved to the states.

Starting Charter Business

Pat left Beef Island shortly before Dick did. She went back to St. Croix to prepare for the arrival of their first baby and to find a place for the family to live. Dick soon joined her there and together they built a successful charter business, with Pat running the office and Dick the boats. The business began with the *Ay Ay*, which lasted 42 years in that service and got Dick his start in the multihull design business.

Before sailing each morning, Dick scurried around loading supplies and guests. A key part of the routine was a visit from Dick's friend, Ted Dale. Ted was originally from Philadelphia but had moved to St. Croix and become somewhat of an island fixture. He was the local Heineken distributor—a job he took for fun, not money. Some mornings, he'd drive down to the wharf in his 1935 Rolls Royce Town Car and deliver ten cases of beer to the *Ay Ay*. *"That always impressed the guests."*

Then, off they'd go. *"We took passengers five miles out to Buck Island. At the time, it was privately owned. Later, it became a national monument owned by the U.S. government. Buck Island has easily accessible reefs for snorkeling, along with a beautiful beach."*

Dick would pull up to the beach and show his passengers how to use snorkels. They'd have lunch under the cockpit awning, and then sail to the reef a short distance away. About fifty percent of Dick's clients never snorkeled before. He had to give them lessons. The best way to get them started was to use an inflatable mattress with a face hole. They'd put the mask on and put their face in the water. Dick would tow them around; show them the best part of the reef.

At the end of the day, Dick was everybody's hero. He remembers always getting a big thank you. *"Some would thank me for the best day of their lives."* Word spread, and Dick's reputation grew.

Of course, there were other charter boats and big competition for passengers. Dick remembers one skipper who was so hungry for business that he started to pass himself off as Dick Newick. *"Passengers would come down the dock and ask if he was Dick Newick. He'd say sure and let people call him Dick all day."*

Just as Dick himself had been envious of the man in Florida, who had been the inspiration for Dick's dream—*"I liked the boat and the life he had built for himself"*—now Dick found himself being envied by others, including some of his very rich and very accomplished clientele. *"People would come into the office and make a reservation and come back very, very happy. Sometimes I'd come alongside the wharf or row them ashore, several times I'd be rowing and the guy would say, 'Dick I'd give anything to do what you are doing.' I didn't have the heart to say, 'Would you give up your vacation home, your Mercedes, your social status and income? Would you give up all that for 80 hour work weeks and not an awful lot to put in the bank?' Of course they wouldn't, but it was a really nice daydream."*

Trine and Trice are Built with Partner Charles Case

Soon Dick was able to expand his fleet, which required capital. Dick was making a profit, but not enough to finance more boats on his own. The money would have to come from an investor, and lucky for Dick, he found a very good one.

The first boat they built was *Trine*, a 32-foot trimaran. Charles E. Case bought the materials and Dick provided the labor. *"Charles, who had lost his father on the Titanic, went to work for Mr. Eastman—as he referred to him— when he was just 15 years old. He made $15 a week."* At the time that Dick met him, Charles was retired, wintering in St. Croix, and still serving on the board of Eastman Kodak.

He offered to buy the material, if Dick provided the labor. The arrangement was that Charles would use the boat occasionally when he was on the island in the winter-time, and otherwise Dick would be free to charter it. *"He told me if you occasionally have a charter when I'm in town, I can make other arrangements, I'm flexible."*

Charles was well connected. One of his old friends was the gentleman in charge of all the Rockefeller hotels. So, when Lawrence Rockefeller opened his new hotel on Virgin Gorda, *Trine* became part of the three-day weekend festivities. Rockefeller invited two 747s full of his closest friends down to the opening, and I was contracted to be there with my boat. They said, *"If the guests like it we'll probably buy it."*

Trine (*Photo by Fritz Henle*)

Charles and Dick sailed *Trine* over the day before the opening. Charles's old friend came down to the beach to meet them, but he didn't see Charles right away. So, Charles ended up joining Dick and his crew for dinner in the hotel kitchen. *"The guy was mortified when he discovered his friend eating in the kitchen with the help."*

Later as the big ceremony was about to get underway, Dick headed back down to the beach. He was waiting there with the boat, when several of the Rockefeller guests ambled by. They said, *"What's the deal with this funny boat?"* I told them, *"I'm here for the guests."* And, they said, *"We're guests—let's go!"* And so it was that Dick suddenly found himself spending three days sailing with Tom Watson, the head of IBM, plus the chairman of Time Inc., the head of Colliers Inc., and others.

Trine was sold to Lawrence Rockefeller, and Charles and Dick had started plans for a second boat together. Their trimaran *Trice* was in the process when Charles learned he had lung cancer and only a few months to live. He realized that he might not even make it to the launch. Dick remembers his wonderful attitude. He told me, *"I have learned in life that anticipation is better than realization; I'm anticipating this boat and enjoying it thoroughly."*

Trice

Before Charles died, he, Dick and Pat spent three days sailing on *Trine* in picture perfect weather from St. Croix to Virgin Gorda, St. John, and back to St. Croix. They shared the pleasure of each other's company feeling no need to fill the void with more than a little conversation.

Preaching Multihulls

In those years, multihulls were new and Dick spent much of his time convincing first-time clients to give multihulls a try. He vividly remembers the February months when the New York yacht club men with their red pants and blue blazers would descend on St. Croix. Their first question upon entering his office was always, *"What do you have to offer?"* Dick would go through the options, and they'd always say, *"Well, we're not interested in those multihulls"*. Dick would ask if they'd ever tried one, to which they'd reply, *"No and I never want to."* I'd say, *"You remind me of a ten year old boy who says he's never going to have anything to do with girls."* That usually got their attention.

Dick said that a few multihull designers had a tendency to over-promise and under deliver, giving multihulls and those who designed them a bad rap. To counter this attitude, Dick always promised that if they took one of his boats out and weren't completely happy, at the end of the day they'd get their money back. Nobody ever came back for their money. *"I didn't want them to fall down and worship multihulls. I just wanted them to know that there were better boats out there."*

Dick's sales pitch didn't end once he got them aboard. One of the great benefits of being in the charter business is that he had a captive audience for his ideas. For several hours, he could extol the virtues of multi-hulls. *"They couldn't' walk away from my tirade,"* he jokes, admitting that his message was very subtle, something along the gentle lines of, *"Take another look at multihulls."* He says it was sort of a fun challenge to take very wealthy, very opinionated, very respected people—like Supreme Court Justice Goldberg who kept finishing all of Dick's sentences for him, New York Mayor John Lindsey who refused to wear a hat or sunscreen—and show them the light. *"Not like an evangelical preacher. I'd try to be more subtle, like the Quakers."*

His strategy worked, with an added benefit. Not only did he get traditional sailors to appreciate multihulls, he got them to *buy* multihulls. His multihulls. *"Just like a 10-year-old boy putting his arm around a girl. Things change."*

A case in point is Fairleigh Dickenson Jr., who became Dick's friend. Becton/Dickinson was a leading medical supply house that got its start building syringes in Dick's hometown of Rutherford, New Jersey. Fairleigh, called Dick by friends and family, had taken over the company from his father. *"My grandfather had been on the board of his father's bank."* In St. Croix, Dick Dickinson owned 300 acres of the island and two hotels. Dick Newick describes him as a quiet philanthropist. When Dickinson first sailed *Trice*, he told Dick that he thought it was a great boat and asked if it was in production. Dick said that as a matter of fact a Maine boat builder who had recently chartered it for a week was interested in reproducing it, to which Dickinson responded, *"Well, I'll order the first one."* This initial investment got a series of seven started. In addition to buying the first and second of the series, Dickinson ended up buying the original as well. He saw that Dick's partner wasn't a good fit and an arrangement was made to buy him out, under an agreement that was similar to the one Dick had with Charles. Both of the Maine built boats were big earners for Dickinson's hotels, a fact that Newick is proud of. Part of the trimarans' success came from one of Dickinson's charter captains, and superb calypso singer, Llewelyn Westerman. The guests not only got to sail to Buck Island, but were entertained by Llewlyn's singing.

The Charter Crew

Another point of pride for Dick was his charter business crew and the fact that, while so many young immigrants got their start in St. Croix working illegally, the ones Dick employed eventually became U.S. citizens. Some worked for Dick for that purpose alone. Others worked for Dick because they shared his passion for sailing—and for speed. A standout among them was Bomba, a native Cruzan.

While Dick continued his multihull enthusiasm, he did eventually add what he calls *"a wreck of a sloop"* to his fleet. He did this, not so much to bow to popular demand, but to acquire the skippers who were part of the deal and maybe convert them.

Dick purchased the dilapidated Tortola sloop, *Northstar*, for $1,000, a bargain he figured because the boat came with Bomba, who had the reputation of being the most famous sailor in the West Indies. Shortly there-after, Bomba became the skipper of *Ay Ay*.

Together they were a great combination: *Ay Ay* could move fast and Bomba was up for the challenge. Because of the boat's speed, skippers usually had to move quickly to keep things under control. This could have posed a problem for Bomba. He walked with a strong limp, the result of a fall down a hatch in his younger years, which dislocated his knee. An orthopedic surgeon who sailed with Dick one day said it had never properly set. *"He told me that if he ever stops walking, his knee is going to seize up. That's probably why Bomba never stopped moving."* But, Dick says that he never saw Bomba move fast, mostly because he never had to. The beauty in watching him work the boat was that he anticipated everything.

He was also an incredibly dedicated and loyal employee, who loved to sail. *"He called me every day at 6:30 a.m. and asked if there was any business that day. Even if things were slow and I had given him the day off, he'd call."* This was partly because Dick paid his employees whether they sailed or not, which was rare in the industry. The lady who owned *North Star* had been taking whatever business came and, with no advertising, very little business came in. She charged $35 per day for the boat. She paid the skipper $5. For Bomba and Arthur Connor, who came to work for Dick at the same time, it was a hit or miss proposition. Bomba had three kids; Arthur had six. It wasn't long before both of them were making $100 per week with Dick and the steady stream of work his business produced.

When business was slow, Dick would hire out his boats for odd jobs, ideal for torpedo testing with the Navy, for example. *"We could go out in a sailboat with listening equipment. Because there was no engine, they could listen for the torpedo propeller."* Or, his crew would help move a boat to shore. *"We would haul out onto a beach with a few rollers, block and tackle, pulley and ropes, with Bomba and four or five other guys pulling. I'd say, 'Bomba, it's not gonna go. We need more power.' And, he'd say, 'Chief, she's got to come.' And he was always right."*

In the off-season—usually May and June—Dick's crew worked with Wally Galloway, the boat shop's manager, on whatever new design was under construction.

In July, August, and September—the height of hurricane season—the crew helped to secure the fleet. If there was a hurricane warning, boats were moved to a narrow mangrove channel for protection. They were tied up there to ride out the storm. Otherwise, there was a 70% chance of losing the boats. This was easy enough to do in the early years when there weren't many yachts on the island, but it became harder over the years as the competition grew; owners were vying for sheltered spots. *North Star* was lost in 1989 during Hurricane Hugo. Dick had a total of twelve boats of his design on the island by 1989—half in charter and half in private use. Hugo reduced that number to six.

The First Racers

Dick's fleet now included three boats—*Ay Ay*, *Trine*, and *Northstar*. The steady stream of business allowed him to pay the bills and have a little left over for trying out new ideas, a venture he calls non-immediate returns on the investment. One of these was a trimaran named Lark, after Dick and Pat's first daughter.

Launched in 1962, *Lark* wasn't built for the charter business; she was too small—and too fast. Dick built Lark to experiment with speed. He was after more horsepower, which meant he needed more sail area. But more sail area would tip a boat, unless the boat had enough weight to keep it upright. Dick figured he needed about 200 pounds of crew on the windward hull for the sail area he was planning. *"You can put a 200 pound friend out on the rail which will help keep the boat right side up, but I didn't necessarily want to feed or listen to a 200 pound friend every time I sailed."*

Lark (Photo by Fritz Henle)

While developing *Lark*, Dick mailed a sketch to Arthur Piver, a pioneer in the field, for feedback. He didn't get much in the way of advice, except for a single sentence: *"you might consider giving the ama more displacement."* While Dick was disappointed with the brief note, he soon realized that Piver was absolutely right. *"It was a common mistake in those days."*

As a possible solution, Dick experimented with *"dagger foils"* in the outer hulls to provide lift like an airplane wing in water. *"Fifteen or twenty years later, the French* discovered that idea and they were shocked they hadn't invented it first."

Dick doesn't take credit for inventing it either; he does, however, take credit for improving it. He tried Ash, Douglas Fir, and fiberglass, which promptly snapped off, like carrots. *"That proved to me that they were working, so I started using more exotic materials. Finally, I started using carbon fiber. Looking at the boat from the front, I started with the foils inclined 27 degrees, then 30 degrees. More degrees equal more lift."* There was no center board so the *"dagger foils"* also prevented leeway.

Dick says that *Lark* did over 20 knots when things were right, and he only capsized her once. It was a great educational tool—and a whole lot of fun to sail. He sold the boat to David Rockefeller for his place on St. Barts.

"Now, I give my trimarans more displacement, my catamarans more beam, so they can carry more payload and more sail. In the old days I could do 20 knots; now, my boats are pushing 30 knots, which is very fast for a non-million dollar yacht. Most people have to spend a lot of money to go that fast."

"Too many of today's races have turned into a contest to see who can spend the most money on high tech advancements - race to buy first place." This led to sponsorship—boats covered with corporate logos—not Dick's idea of fun.

In the early years, however, when Dick first got involved in racing, the spotlight was on the salty skippers, rather than the sponsors. The glory—and lots of it—went to the sailors who had the skill, the stamina, and the sheer guts to cross the Atlantic in boats sometimes so small that, for reviewer Martin Luray, brought to mind the image of a potato chip floating on the ocean.

Tom Follet

Dick had raced a bit back in college, but didn't think of himself as an accomplished racer. He sailed *Ay Ay* on St. Croix, but very informally, as the local yacht club's annual race consisted primarily of 60-foot schooners. *"I can often remember coming in an hour ahead of the second boat in a forty mile race."*

Dick thought about racing more competitively, and the one he most wanted to enter was the OSTAR. The OSTAR, a single-handed transatlantic race run by the Royal Western Yacht Club of Plymouth, England, covered 3,000 hard, solo miles windward across the North Atlantic to Newport, Rhode Island. It started in 1960 with Blondie Hasler and Francis Chichester's solo race sponsored by the London's Observer newspaper, to be continued every four years. According to Dick, it was an ideal test for new ideas in the 60s and 70s with a minimum of rules. *"I always wanted to do that race, but I never had the opportunity, partly because it was hard to convince Pat it was a good idea."*

Tom Follet would be the first to enter the OSTAR with a Dick Newick designed boat in 1968. Tom, an expert seaman, said, if you can build it, I'll race it. The trick, of course, was getting it built. Or, more to the point, paying for the materials. In other words, the boat needed an owner—someone willing to buy a boat they'd probably never use, a boat for speed, not the usual pleasure, a pure racer.

Cheers

In those days it was possible for a husband and wife with a passion for multihulls and a love of the sport to be the sole sponsors of a winning boat. That husband, wife team was Jim and Tootie Morris. The boat they sponsored was *Cheers*. They were in it for the sheer joy of competition, for the privilege of becoming part of the team.

Dick and Pat met Jim and Tootie, (Mary C. Sinclaire,) in St. Croix when they came to visit Tootie's parents, who had a winter home on the beach. Her parents often chartered *Ay Ay* and Dick got to know Jim and Tootie when they came along for a sail. It was aboard the *Ay Ay* one day that Dick shared his plans for entering a boat in the OSTAR with Follet as skipper. Dick originally was looking for 12 investors at $1,000 apiece. Jim and Tootie thought that would be too much trouble, and they offered to put up all the money.

Tootie christening Cheers
(*photo by Fritz Henle*)

73

In the end, their total investment was in the area of $32K, for the boat and all the expenses associated with the race, what Dick refers to as 'the project'—including travel expenses to ensure that the Newicks, Morris' and Tom's wife, Priscilla would be on hand for the start in Plymouth, England, to be joined by the four Newick, Morris children at the finish of the race in Newport, Rhode Island.

The First Pure Racer

Dick's St. Croix shop was in a dilapidated truck garage used in the 1930's Civilian Conservation Corps at a sugar plantation called Estate Little Princess. *Cheers* emerged from the garage—the birthplace of other designs—and into multihull history. One of 34 starters that year, *Cheers* became the first American boat to complete the OSTAR, finishing third overall against many much bigger boats.

The editors of Latitude 38 had written that Dick *"had broken into the limelight by designing one of the most unique craft ever to do any ocean race."*

Cheers was so unusual that the Royal Western Yacht Club committee rejected the entry request with cordial, but firm letters . . .

The first, dated August 18, 1967 reads:

Dear Mr. Follett,

I fear that your figures and explanations have done little to revise our anxieties about your proposed entry. In particular the figures for the lifting of the two hulls do not seem to take into account the position of the masts, and therefore the C of E of the sails in relation to the two hulls. Having considered the matter carefully the Committee are of the opinion that because of the very real risk of a capsize when this craft is sailed single-handed, and also because of the too restricted accommodation for the crew, this vessel cannot in any sense be considered suitable for single-handed ocean crossing. Therefore to accept the entry would not contribute to the object of the race, and we regret we are unable to do so, unless and until we can be satisfied on the first point by performance and on the second by actual inspection.

I return your entry fee herewith.

Yours sincerely,
Terrence W.B. Shaw

There were more letters exchanged and each time the rejection was repeated. It was eventually decided that the only way to prove that Cheers could handle the North Atlantic was for Tom to sail solo to England from St. Croix, U.S. Virgin Islands. Which is what he did.

Race committee members met Tom, inspected the boat, and eventually allowed her official entry into the 1968 OSTAR.

Tom Follett finished third against the two winners, much bigger monohulls. His was the first Proa entered with nine trimarans and three catamarans. Most of the multihulls and many of the traditional boats didn't finish. Geoffrey Williams, on the winning 57 foot monohull, Sir Thomas Lipton, had a decided advantage with a high-powered radio to receive meteorologist weather reports from early model computer systems. He sailed north away from a storm that hammered the other contenders, with an estimated gain of 300 miles. Weather routing was temporarily banned from future races. Multihulls were inching into international racing, and Cheers helped lead the way.

In the forward to the book, *Project Cheers*, written by Tom, Jim, and Dick, H.G (Blondie) Hasler wrote:

> The 1968 Cheers project will stand as a perfect example of the sort of thing that the Single-Handed Transatlantic Race was designed to encourage. I don't know which to admire the most: the extreme unorthodoxy of the boat's conception, or the strength and simplicity of her construction; or perhaps her wild good looks; or the efficiency with which she was tested, modified, re-tested and then proof-tested in that extraordinary passage from St. Croix to Gosport; or Tom Follett's impeccable seamanship allied to his rudimentary ocean-going inventory. I think most great seamen have chosen

to use a minimum of equipment: we have another Slocum here. Next we can appreciate the team's sportsmanship and good manners in dealing with the Royal Western Yacht Club, and for that matter the responsible attitude of Jack Odling-Smee and his hard pressed Race Committee in first rejecting this apparently frivolous entry, and then being able to change their minds gracefully when presented with fresh evidence.

Cheers is really a very small boat, as anyone who got into her cabin can testify. The route which she took, or was forced to take, is in my opinion a slow one which would normally add several days to any boat's time. I think she did superbly to finish third, and to better Taberly's 1964 record passage. Every part of the Cheers project seems to have set a standard of excellence that we can now look on and marvel at.

H.G. Hasler
Curdridge Hampshire
3rd June 1969

In the process of building *Cheers*, Dick had contacted his old idol L. Francis Herreshoff, who agreed to make a gooseneck for *Cheers*. *"To have a piece of Herreshoff designed and built hardware on your boat was fantastic."* However, it eventually became overdue. Herreshoff wrote to say that he was too old to do it, a bit too shaky. Dick admits it wouldn't have worked anyway, and the loss gave him a chance to come up with an idea that ended up working even better.

Cheers was equipped with a radio receiver for shortwave government weather forecasts, which worked fairly well in the middle of the ocean and along the coast. *"Tom would know when there was a hurricane approaching."* The radio did not allow for communication to shore, however. *"The only way to know where they were is if they were reported seen at sea by a passing ship. In Newport, we'd go out and look at the horizon, strain our eyes in the fog when Tom was expected to finish."* It was an exciting day when—straining their eyes in the fog—Jim and Dick witnessed history in the making as *Cheers* made its way into the harbor.

The book, *Project Cheers,* tells the whole story.

In a letter to Dick from L. Francis Herreshoff, dated May 2, 1966, he wrote:

Dear Mr. Newick,

I was very pleased and interested to receive your letter of April 26 about the proa you have been building. I think that you have some very valuable experience during the next few years. But, I cannot help but prophesy that you and other multi-hull designers will eventually go back to the single hull boats, just as they did in Charles II's time, 1660's, and again when my father had started the catamaran rage here in 1876. Perhaps some of you, like my father, will produce some remarkable boats, after your experience with the multihull types.

Yes, I approve of simplicity, and on small sail areas, I certainly like and use boom jaws, and reefing with reef points. Also, for long distance sailing, all those things that can be repaired at sea are best.

I am glad you had a sail on Circe. While she may be the natural development of the sailboats, if it were not for measurement rules, still much improvement in her could be made today. After all, I designed her 37 years ago.

Yours truly,
L. Francis Herreshoff

Cheers: The Retirement Years

Because of the boat's historic significance, Cheers became a museum piece, residing first in St. Croix, then England, then France, until being fully restored by its current owners, Vincent and Nelie Besin. The boat was first donated by Jim and Tootie to the Historic Society in St. Croix, but they didn't have the means to care for her. A more fitting home was found at the Exeter Small Craft Museum, where Cheers was on display for more than a decade.

Cheers was eventually moved by Daniel Charles, a nautical historian who was living in France at the time. He and Nigel Irons, one of the leading multihull designers in the world, collaborated on a nautical museum project in La Rochelle, France, where Charles served as curator. Cheers was cut in two, shipped from England to France, and rebuilt for display. Years later, the Besins, who owned one Dick Newick trimaran and were working with Dick on a second, a proa design that would take them around the world, met Daniel Charles, saw *Cheers*, and fell in love. *Cheers* was showing her age when Vincent and Nelie offered to move her to the South of France where they intended to preserve her. The couple spent five years and 5,000 hours of their spare time rebuilding her. They were instrumental in having *Cheers* named a *"monument historique"* by the French landmarks committee—the first multihull ever to wear the distinction. "To *think that I designed and built in St. Croix a French historical monument is really funny, but I'm getting used to the idea."*

When the restoration was complete, Vincent and Nelie threw a launch party. Three hundred people—including seven owners of Dick's boats—turned out. Dick says the Besins went to a lot of trouble, laid out the history of *Cheers* in several rooms of their home and organized a traditional Polynesian launch in which the boat is carried to the water.

The Racing Years: Three Cheers

Throughout the 1970s, Dick's boats featured prominently in competitions: the Round the Isle of Wight Race, the Multihull Bermuda Race, the Round Britain Race, and, of course, the coveted OSTAR. He became a major player in the evolution of multihulls from early plywood boats in the 1960s, which were not very fast and not very pretty, to the next generation of round-bottom, cold-molded boats in the 1970s, which were pretty well engineered in what he calls "a caveman sort of way."

3 Cheers (*Photo by Fritz Henle*)

It was during this highly creative period of his life, however, that Dick became more aware of his lack of formal training. *"When I'm playing with boats, I miss a technical education. However, if I had persevered at Michigan, I would have learned everything that couldn't be done, and not having learned that, I went ahead and did what couldn't be done."*

Where did his inspiration come from, if not from a classroom and a college degree? He often jokes—only half facetiously, he says—that it came from a previous life. People ask, *"Where do you get these funny ideas? Well,"* I tell them, *"I must have been a Polynesian canoe builder in a previous life."*

Or, perhaps a short order cook, as the tendency to compare Dick's boats to food continued. *Cheers* had been described as a potato chip floating on the ocean. Four years later, *Three Cheers* was born—and with it came comparisons to, of all things, banana fritters.

Jim Morris, Dick Newick & Tom Follet
(*Photo by Fritz Henle*)

Three Cheers

Three Cheers, so named because the original Cheers team had reunited for another go at the OSTAR, was a radical 46-foot trimaran design. And, the last major design to come out of the St. Croix boatyard.

"It *was a much more ambitious project. Twice as heavy. Twice as expensive.*" The old, decrepit government garage wasn't big enough to accommodate the entire boat. Instead, it had to be built in stages. The hulls were built individually in the garage and then stored outside, where the boat was eventually assembled. *"We kept plastic to throw over the boat when it rained during the winter months."*

Different people worked on the construction at different times. Dave Dana offered technical support. Ian Major was on hand. Progress was quick, thanks in part to a reliable supplier who had worked with Dick on *Cheers* four years prior. *"There were no glitches. We put the boat in the water several months before she needed to go to England."*

And, then the glitch emerged. *Three Cheers* was a yawl instead of a sloop. She didn't have self-steering. This was before the days of electronic self-steering, when wind vanes—which Blondie Hasler helped to popularize and perfect—were used. But, they were not good on multihulls because apparent wind varied excessively when surfing down a wave. *"You can be doing 10 knots, get a wave under the stern, and then be doing 20 knots, which changes apparent wind direction. It throws off the ability to self-steer because self-steering is dependent upon wind direction."*

"With a yawl, you use the small mizzen back aft to help steer the boat. I thought that would be enough." In addition, Dick added a centerboard to balance the boat, which worked so well with *Cheers*, but she still didn't self-steer the way she should have. During trials, they kept trying to do things that would make it easier to self-steer.

Dick says they came up with a lot of little fixes, but no major fix. In the end, it cost them the race.

"We had the fastest boat in the race, I thought. But Tom was forced to slow the pace, trim the sails to self-steer, compromise his speed, in order to take care of other things. It was a disappointment to place 5th."

Jim and Tootie Morris found themselves owning another boat built for racing, not for pleasure. They would have been happy being absentee owners, leaving it in Dick's capable hands, but Dick and Pat were planning to leave St. Croix.

Mike McMullen, an English sailor who had finished the OSTAR two days after Tom, winning in his class, had sailed *Three Cheers* in Plymouth before the race and loved it. Dick describes Mike McMullen as the English version of Tom Follet with a more outgoing personality. *"He was the son of a Royal Navy captain, and the nephew of a Royal Navy admiral. Mike himself was a tough Royal Marine commando. His specialty was arctic and desert warfare. Everybody loved him. Tough, vivacious, played guitar, a happy companion."*

Mike was to visit an American cousin that he'd never met. Building and campaigning the boat had cost Jim $32K, so they sought a buyer with that kind of money. Jim asked, *"Who's your American cousin?"* Mike didn't know him at all, but said, *"His name is Paul Mellon."* At the time, Paul Mellon may have been the richest man in the United States. His father had given the country the National Art Gallery. Paul was a horse racing enthusiast.

Jim suggested that he might want to buy the boat. *"Tell your cousin Paul that you could be the jockey on his latest horse, Three Cheers."* Jim's suggestion paid off.

Three Cheers headed to England for the Round Britain race and so did Dick. The Mellon deal included travel expenses for Dick to supervise improvements to self-steering at the Mashfords' Cremyll boatyard. Jim paid his way and came along to help. Dick remembers that there were seven people named Mashford working with him and that the boatyard had a sawmill, foundry, cabinet shop, technical shop, and machine shop. Their beautiful, antiquated shop and location were featured in one of Latitude 38's publications. Dick and Jim ended up behind schedule, so they decided to work over the Easter holiday weekend. *"We were given keys to every shop in the complex—a testament to the Mashfords' trust in us."* They spent most of the weekend working, but managed to attend Mike's wedding on Saturday in Cornwall—a very formal, very military affair. *"I saw a lot of gold braids. Jim and I wore blue blazers. Everyone else, not in uniform, was in top hats and tails."*

With improved self-steering, Mike at the helm, and co-skipper Martin Read, *Three Cheers* placed second in the 1974 Round Britain Race, beaten by only one hour, eleven minutes by the 70-foot British Oxygen.

Mike and his new wife, Elizabeth, actually used *Three Cheers* as a pleasure boat, cruising to the coast of Spain in 1975. Elizabeth, affectionately known to friends as "Lizzie," recounted their adventure, along with Mike's love for the boat, in Yachting World magazine, *"Beauty is in the eye of the beholder and my husband Mike believes that Three Cheers is the most beautiful thing ever created."* Lizzie also admired the boat, though not to the same extent as Mike, and she was obviously amused by the comments that *Three Cheers* drew, *"She is, I admit, aesthetically beautiful—though she has been described as a 'bleedin' aeroplane,' a yellow pancake and a banana fritter."*

Sadly, Mike lost his wife, Lizzie, just before the 1976 OSTAR. Helping to get the boat ready for the race, she died when an electric sander fell into the water and she reached to grab it. The Newicks, along with so many others, were devastated by the loss of Lizzie who was a close friend. Mike, naturally, was distraught. Both Dick and Tom were ready to take Mike's place for the race, but they didn't feel it was quite right to make the offer. They both knew Mike should make the choice. *"Tom and I were back up skippers who had done the 500 solo miles to qualify for the race. But, we didn't want to ask Mike if he wanted one of us to take over. We didn't say anything. We knew he wanted to do it."* Mike and *Three Cheers* entered the race, and disappeared somewhere in the North Atlantic Ocean.

Jim Brown writing for Sail Magazine, spoke with Dick at the time, when speculation about Mike's whereabouts was at its height. Dick told Jim, *"It begins to look as though we just may never see Mike McMullen again. He hasn't even been sighted since the start, and I know he was going to race the northern route. Nobody could survive those cold waters for long in a capsized multihull, or even less in a life raft. Sailing single-handed of course gives a better chance for collision...like with an iceberg."*

Losing Mike and *Three Cheers* during the 1976 OSTAR was a huge blow to the Newicks, and to everyone who knew him. It was their first experience with the tragedy and heartbreak that is sometimes the hallmark of tough competition.

Moving to Martha's Vineyard

While Dick's reputation was growing, the island paradise his family called home was in decline. And, Dick was faced with a tough decision. He had moved to St. Croix because of its climate, which he describes as the best in the world. *"It never goes below 68, never goes above 90. Pretty good with trade winds keeping it cool and making it fun to sail. The best place to sail in the world."* But, it was no longer safe.

During the time that Dick and Pat lived on St. Croix, Dick says that white people made up only about 10% of the island's population. Racial tensions started to escalate in the 1960's, and eventually reached the point where Dick felt it was not safe for his children. One source of animosity was land. In the 1950's, Dick says, native islanders were selling their land for $100 an acre. They didn't realize its value until later. As they watched their former land prices going up, so did their resentment. Along with that problem was the lack of job opportunities. Tensions grew and violence began within weeks after Newicks left St. Croix.

It was with mixed feelings that Dick and Pat finally said goodbye to friends and to the three schools they helped to establish. They sold their charter business and waterfront office lease in 1972. Chase Manhattan Bank rented their house for Pat's cousin, an officer with the bank. He would live in their unique, beautiful home designed by their friend, Tom Counter, with a Caribbean view stretching to St. Thomas, St. John, and the British Virgin Islands, until it sold two years later.

By then, Newicks owned and operated four day charter boats, the catamaran *Ay Ay*, a 47 foot power boat named Providencia, a Newick designed trimaran called *Tricia*, and *North Star*, the native sloop.

Danish friends of Dick's planned to take a year's sabbatical in Tanzania, and offered their house in Vordingborg, Denmark to him. The Newicks planned to stay for a year. Dick enjoyed his new sense of freedom. He had plenty of time to design, or just think. Pat did not. She was busy home-schooling Lark and Val, then 11 and 13, who had a difficult time entering the local school system in the middle of the term. It was an awkward age socially when their Danish friends spoke a little English, and then carried on conversations in their more familiar language. The kids felt isolated and unhappy. Pat wasn't happy because the kids weren't happy.

Within three months Dick's friends decided to return to Denmark and Newicks were ready to return to the States. They spent Christmas with Pat's family in Minnesota, then explored the Chesapeake area which appealed to them, until they discovered how prevalent racial divisions still were among the school kids. The search for a perfect mix of climate and consciousness continued. It ended on Martha's Vineyard.

Karl Riley, an old friend from St. Croix days who had partnered with Dick on the trimaran, Lark, spent his summers on the Vineyard. He had purchased 20 acres at $60/acre in the early 1960s, divided it into 1.7 acre lots, and sold them to friends. The Newicks bought a lot for $2,000 in the late 60's, sight unseen. At the time, they thought of the land as a vacation campsite, not as a potential home. But, that changed in 1973, when they saw their investment for the first time and decided to build on it.

Dick designed a simple, rustic house of rough sawn pine. While it was being built, the Newick family rented the second floor of a lovely old home owned by the local health food store proprietor Milton Wend, who had recently lost his wife. He was both fascinating and opinionated, recounting stories of working with the Wright Brothers and offering Pat endless advice as she cooked meals in their shared kitchen. Soon the family moved to their new home. Both daughters enrolled in a local school until Lark went to boarding school in Vermont. Val decided to stay on the Vineyard.

Dick focused on design work and occasionally built a boat.

By this time, Dick Newick's designs were big news. The press coverage of the 1968 OSTAR and the publication of *Project Cheers* definitely piqued people's interest. The old,

"Well, we're not interested in those multihulls," from Dick's St. Croix days was slowly being replaced with *"Say, I'd like to try one."*

Nick Friedberg was one of the first. After reading *Project Cheers*, Nick decided that *"he wanted one of those."* He got in touch with Dick on Martha's Vineyard and Nick's boat became the first proa that Dick designed in his new location. Dick spent three summers tweaking the design of Nick's 34-foot day-boat, but still didn't think it was quite right for Nick, who was not a natural sailor. In the end, Nick called it off. *"He said that it was nobody's fault but it wasn't working and said I could have it. Another real gentleman."*

Before the Newicks left St. Croix, John Olin and his wife had come and chartered *Tricia, Dick's 36-foot trimaran,* with Inglore Westerman as skipper. John had purchased a *Hobie* 16 catamaran, which had very similar amas. He liked *Tricia* and bought a set of plans. Olin scaled down Dick's drawings and built a 23-foot main hull to combine with his *Hobie* 16 rig using the hulls as amas. The result was a new class called the *Tremolino.* In Dick's mind it was an inexpensive way for an owner of a *Hobie* 16 to have a trimaran that could sleep two people, in very Spartan conditions. There was a cockpit that was comfortable for four and the boat could do 18 knots. John sold about a hundred of them. When asked if he'd use the term hybrid to describe the mixing and matching of boat components, Dick responded, *"No, we just called it a Tremolino and let people figure it out."* At one point, John and Dick got permission to sail along in a Hobie 16 National Championship. The *Tremolino* was twice as heavy and twice as wide, which meant it had more sail carrying power than a *Hobie* 16. The *Tremolino* finished in the middle of the fleet. "But the Hobie company was not the least bit interested in what we were doing. We were detracting from their business."

Gulf Streamer

The first major design project to come out of Martha's Vineyard was the 60-foot trimaran *Gulf Streamer* for Phil Weld. The project began in 1973, as did Nick Friedberg's proa. Unlike Nick's boat, however, *Gulf Streamer* made it off the drawing board, and into the water—for the 1974 Round Britain Race.

Phil, an experienced sailor, had chartered Dick's boats in St. Croix and raced Round Britain on a Kelsall trimaran. He had a boat under construction at the time he contacted Dick on the Vineyard. He had reservations about the design and was looking for a second opinion. Dick headed up to Gloucester to take a look. The boat, designed by Ray Hunt and modeled after his International 110, was being built by Alan Vaitses. Dick could see why some folks were telling Phil it wasn't quite right and Dick struggled with what to do. He didn't want to insult a fellow designer— who happened to be one of the most famous alive. But, he wanted to be fair to Phil. The boat was scrapped and a new *Gulf Streamer* was conceived.

Martin Luray (Rudder Magazine, May 1974) writes, *"Weld, who is without a doubt one of the world's premier multihull sailors, had asked for a boat that could range the world quickly and comfortably with four on board, yet be easily handled by a crew of two in the Round Britain Race or by a crew of one (Weld) in the next Singlehanded TransAtlantic Race."*

When the project was complete, Dick was confident that the boat would deliver. He told Luray, "*I think they can be assured of doing their 200 miles a day average with a short crew, and, as far as racing is concerned, I don't know of anything that can stay with her. I think she'll sail circles around anything that's afloat."*

Writing for *Rudder* Magazine (May 1974) in the article, "Gulf Streamer Hull Design", Martin Luray explains that the layup of the Gulf Streamers hulls are unconventional:

> Newick used a system of foam core construction, in which he was able to design a female mold for his 60-foot main hull off which the two 44-foot amas could also be pulled. All of the hulls were built in two halves and then joined. For core material Newick used Airex PVC foam with a layup cross-section of gelcoat-mat-roving-mat-roving-mat, then Airex and, on the inside, mat-roving-mat-roving. In some areas of stress, unidirectional glass fibers are used, and to stiffen the rudder skeg, carbon fibers are used.
>
> Layup samples using various combinations of mat, roving and core thicknesses were both lab-tested and subjected to scrutiny by Newick, Weld and Vaitses. In one such experiment last summer conducted al fresco under two trees in the yard

area, the scale built up to 325 pounds of stress, causing Weld to comment, *"This is the equivalent of hitting Ram Island at how many knots? Isn't that what we're really worried about with the amas?"*

Newick explained, *"We've got to have an awful lot of stiffness on the ends of those cantilevered amas, not just for local impact. When they are buried in a beam sea, with the whole surface subject to compression and sheer, the sea is going to try to break the bows off."*

The boat made headlines, first for its form but also for its Spartan style—which was fast becoming Dick's trademark. The press was curious to see how Dick had improved upon his earlier successes—*Cheers* and *Three Cheers*. Martin Luray, writing for Rudder Magazine (May 1974), talked with Dick about the design similarities and differences. Dick compared *Gulf Streamer* to *Three Cheers*, saying that *Gulf Steamer* has open decks but that *"basically, however, the rig is the same—double headsail ketch. But we don't have a mizzenmast. We have an unusual mizzen that's fixed to the backstay top and bottom but it's hoisted on its own jackstay. It's primarily for balance. Three Cheers rarely sailed with a jib—mostly staysail, main and mizzen."*

Again, the critics searched for comparisons. Whereas *Cheers* had previously been described as a potato chip floating on the ocean and *Three Cheers* as banana fritters, Martin Luray took a more serious tone, saying that parallels to Dick's design aesthetic could be found both in nature and architecture—recalling that he once overheard someone describe *Three Cheers* as a manta ray with armpits. For Luray, *Gulf Streamer* was more bird-like in appearance, given as he says, its three sets of 'wings' on each side. As it turned out, it was exactly the look that Dick was after. He told Luray, *"Wind is about 1/800th the density of water. So I was not concerned with windage, as much as keeping the wings as low as possible for aesthetic reasons and as high as possible to lessen potential water drag. And so the gull-wing shape used on Three Cheers evolved."*

In the end, Luray writes, Dick believed that aesthetic considerations and form can be put to functional use at sea. When asked by Luray if the wing connectors were more aesthetic than functional, Dick replied: *"They were given that shape for hydrodynamic reasons. Occasionally, they have to go through wave tops, which they must do as easily as possible. But they also must have strength."*

Spartan Style

Luray marveled at the Spartan accommodations of *Gulf Streamer*. He writes, *"...for all of her size, [Gulf Streamer] has no provisions for carrying ice, and what electrics there are, mainly for wind instruments, logs and lights, operate off a pair of standard 12V batteries. Below there are provisions for bunking six in built-in berths. Two longitudinally placed built-in benches serve as seating at a plywood table; the skipper's quarters contain a large built-in chart table, stool and two-burner Optimus stove for the galley, and that is it. Up forward, just short of the forepeak, there is a simple head and locker area as wide as* the main hull (5 ½ feet). There is no expensive teak to keep up on Gulf Streamer."

In Luray's article, Dick put the simplicity into easy-to-understand, layman's terms, *"There's a double bunk that's big enough for one in comfort or two in love."*

It was Martin Luray, as well, who perhaps first pointed out that boats of this Spartan sort can only be built with the "acquiescence" of their owner-skippers—Tom Follett, Phil Weld, who themselves are Spartans, according to Luray. He writes, *"It is rare, Newick admits, to find a man like Tom Follett who could make do with a hot meal every 24 hours and 25 gallons of water on a Trans-Atlantic race."*

Design Philosophy

Jim Brown would write later in a feature on *Third Turtle* (Sail Magazine, May 1977) that Dick is a rare designer, who does not include compromise in his design philosophy. In the article, Dick states his philosophy this way: *"There are three major requirements that most people want in their boats: large accommodations, low cost, and high performance. I tell my clients that they can choose any two of these, from a good designer, and be reasonably assured of getting them—but only two. In my designs I offer the latter two in combination; really high performance at reasonable cost."*

It took Brown a while to understand the reasonable cost promise because of the fact that *Cheers, Three Cheers,* and *Gulf Streamer* were what Brown calls "custom one-off creations." He says, *"Their economy shows only when you compare their cost with that of other vessels on the ocean-racing course."* Dick tells him, *"I like to say that very few of my boats have ever been beaten by anything smaller or cheaper. But just think of what we might accomplish with the budgets of those big ones."*

The article goes on to discuss the subjective nature of *"performance"* in which Dick explains that large accommodations and high performance simply can't co-exist at reasonable cost: *"All the 'room' in a roomy boat just naturally becomes filled up in time with what I like to call modern inconveniences, and that means weight. If the boat is heavy, it has to have wide, deep hulls to carry that weight. Wide, deep, heavy hulls just don't go fast—not fast enough to be deserving of the term 'high performance' in today's language."*

Gulf Streamer was indeed a high performance boat. Phil placed third in the two-person Round Britain. *Gulf Streamer* was ultra sleek but heavy, at least according to Dick who says that it's hard to make a light boat with fiberglass—the material of choice. *"Most of my boats were too heavy."* Still, Phil enjoyed her, even cruised the Caribbean on her with his family.

Next, Phil entered the 1976 OSTAR. It was an exciting time for Dick, with a total of six boats of his designs scheduled to compete for the coveted title (including four *Vals*. *Three Cheers* and *Gulf Streamer* had gone head-to-head in the 1974 Round Britain, with Mike McMullen beating Phil by less than three hours, for second place. The racing

Gulf Streamer

world was looking forward to the rematch, especially the Newicks. But, the mood soon changed. Lizzie's sudden death just days before the race saddened all. The start of the race—ordinarily a festive occasion—was somber, with everyone's hearts going out to Mike. The event was further clouded by the loss of *Gulf Streamer*.

Phil and his crew were enroute to the start, far from land in the middle of the Gulf Stream, when they were toppled by a rogue wave. It's a hazard of the Gulf Stream, according to Dick who says that the mixture of currents and wind can cause waves of up to 50 feet to form, moving at a rate of 30 to 40 miles per hour. *"There's no getting out of the way. Your best bet is to turn the boat and ride it."* Phil was below when it hit. His crew member saw it coming and only had time to yell, "Hang on!" The boat pitch poled. Phil and his crew spent five days at sea in the upside down boat. There was no equipment to right it. They were picked up by a passing ship, about 500 miles north of Bermuda and 500 south of Halifax.

Phil was sad to leave *Gulf Streamer* behind and went back to search for her. The tuna-spotting plane he hired had enough fuel for a 12-hour flight. Phil, Dick and the pilot spent twelve solid hours crisscrossing the blue sky, dodging cotton wad clouds. The visibility was great. At 3,000 feet, they could clearly spot fishing buoys, but no sign of *Gulf Streamer*.

Jim Brown, writing for Sail Magazine (May 1977), reported that months later the boat was found, "*still drifting towards Ireland, playing dead, but intact with full cruising stores aboard. There is ample reason to suspect that the owner and crew would still have been warm and well.*" The boat was in such fine shape that the Russian freighter that found her took her to Odessa and donated her to a sailing club. Later, on a Harvard alumni tour of that part of the world, Phil and Ann missed running into their old boat by just one or two blocks. By the time Phil eventually learned of *Gulf Streamer*'s whereabouts, he had another boat under construction. Dick says, "*When Phil found out, he was very magnanimous. His attitude was She's yours, good luck, and how can I help. He could take that attitude because her replacement was underway.*"

Rogue Wave

The capsize of Gulf Streamer was pivotal in creating the first ocean racer for surviving in while upside down. Rogue Wave was designed for the 1976 OSTAR and built by Gougeon Bros. in Bay City, Michigan, famous for their West epoxy system. Meade Gougeon and Dick collaborated on the technical details, reinforcing the cabin top with 4" honeycomb and installing an escape hatch. Dick would describe Rogue Wave, *"She's one of the few of my boats that you could call a yacht."* Alan Vaitses, Gulf Streamer's builder, agreed when he inspected the boat's interior and proclaimed, *"It's like being inside a Steinway piano."*

Rogue Wave

Also unique to the boat was her skipper, Phil Weld, who, at age 65, would have been the oldest person in the race. Weld was not a 'natural sailor,' and might have been one of the least competitive. He was in the races more for the fun and sport of it compared with the harder edged skippers who tweaked every sail, and made every maneuver to gain speed. When Phil later won the OSTAR with *Moxie*, he was as surprised as anybody, and stepped off the boat looking like he'd been out for an afternoon sail.

Phil had become a member of the Royal Western Yacht Club, so was well aware of the controversies developing after the previous OSTAR races. Some of the competitors felt that they were being eclipsed by corporate sponsored boats and professional skippers. During the debate Phil told the committee that he was building a 60 foot trimaran. *"Will that be a problem?"* They assured him it wouldn't, but soon caved in to pressure and created three different classes for the 1980 race. Phil's boat, aptly named *Rogue Wave* by his wife, Ann, was three feet longer than the maximum allowed in the 40 to 57 foot class. Dick had only seen Phil lose his cool twice, and that was the first.

Some of the French sailors reacted to the new rules and started their own race in 1978 called Route du Rhum, from Saint Malo, France, to Pointe a Pitre, Guadeloupe. Sailing *Rogue Wave*, Phil came in third, but Dick felt he might have won if his new mainsail hadn't blown away costing valuable time in such a close race.

Sadly, that was the year and race where the popular French sailor, Alain Colas disappeared on his trimaran *Manureva*, the former *Pen Duick IV*.

Jim Brown, writing for *Sail* Magazine (May 1977 in the article, "Gulf Streamer Struck by Rare, Freak Wave", describes the rare occurrence that resulted in the loss of Gulf Streamer, on its way to the 1976 OSTAR:

> The *Gulf Streamer* episode demonstrated to all multihull watchers that design alone is no guarantee against capsize; Streamer was one of the longest, widest, toughest, sleekest and most conservatively rigged multihull vessels afloat. She was unceremoniously dumped by a rogue wave at a time and place where the north wall of the Gulf Stream was in a turbulent post-storm state. Such waves are truly rare, but they are coming under the attention of maritime interests because they are known to knock off the greatest ships afloat, the supertankers. Freak waves, like the 40-foot-high, double-crested curler that struck *Streamer*, are now suspected of playing a large part in the so-called mystery of the Bermuda Triangle. Owner-skipper Weld says, *"I feel it was almost as if I'd been struck by lightning."*

The Val Series

It was during the Martha's Vineyard years that Dick created a new class of 31-foot trimarans known as the *Val* Series. *"Anytime you have a half dozen boats, you could call it a class; I use the term loosely."* The first *Val* was launched December 1975.

Harry Morss was among the first to own a *Val*. He had an unusual hobby of documenting the performance of his boats, with instruments of his own creation. An added challenge was the fact that he lived in Marblehead and the harbor was really crowded. He had previously owned two trimarans but he wanted something narrower. A modified *Val* was the perfect solution. *"We knocked 5 feet of beam off what was at the time a 25-foot Val. Only for Harry. I wouldn't have done it for anybody else."*

A graduate of Harvard and MIT, Harry was a quiet, very thoughtful man and a pleasure to be around. He helped set up a graduate studies program at Woods Hole Oceanographic.

Harry's *Val* was named *Galliard*, a French folk dance for three people and a very apt name for a three-hulled boat that danced on water. *"After launching Harry Morss's trimaran, we started serious work on the other Vals, selling one to a Canadian living in England and one to a retiree living in Santa Cruz, California, both of whom came to Martha's Vineyard for a month to have the experience of helping to build their own boat."*

Val

To keep things simple, Dick tried to streamline the construction process and do without fiberglass molds. He knew he was onto something but he didn't persevere. *"I think this is one of my worst qualities; I get an idea and if it isn't an instant success I drop it and move on to something else."* Instead, Dick says the process was eventually perfected by Derrick Kelsall, an Englishman now living in New Zealand, who was the first to finish an OSTAR in a multihull.

In all about 30 *Vals* were built, one in Singapore, a few in Europe, and most in the States. The first six or seven *Vals* had a central cockpit, two akas (cross arms,) and a small aft cabin. *"Later on, I decided those boats were rather flexible. To stiffen up the boat, it would be better to have one single aka for the connecting structure. I called them wing akas. They were deep enough from top to bottom to put a bunk and galley out over the water. That stiffened the structure up greatly. All of the later ones had wing akas, much better boats."*

The original Val

When Harry sold *Galliard* in his later years, he gave all the instruments and his records to Dick. *"Harry's wife told me, Harry spent a lot of time documenting all of this, so that you'd understand it. I never did understand it."* Later on, Dick gave all the equipment to MIT to add to Harry's archives. *"I hope they've been able to sort it out better than I."*

When Harry died, he left Dick $5,000, presumably as compensation for the design. *"I didn't charge him much at the time because I was planning to sell his design as a series. I guess he thought he owed me something more for my time."* Dick used the money to invest in a computer and hull design software to learn computer-aided design.

The Vals and the 1976 OSTAR

The *Vals* made a strong showing in the 1976 OSTAR. It was promising to be a tremendous race for the Newicks — with a total of six boats entered, including four of the new *Val* design (as well as *Three Cheers* and *Gulf Streamer*). It was the first race in the sport's history in which multihulls became a dominant factor, but the race was won by Eric Taberly's 73-foot monohull.

Rory Nugent, who had a hand in building the first half dozen *Vals* with his partner, Ovid Ward, entered one. A couple of young guys from Boston came down every weekend to help Dick and Rory build it. *"They didn't charge us anything. They just wanted to be on ground floor of creating the series. So we loaned the mold to them and they built a boat and one of them, Tom Ryan, entered the OSTAR too."*

Another *Val* in the process of being built was for Canadian sailor, Mike Birch, a serious competitor. Dick didn't know anything about Mike, except that he had grown up in British Columbia and worked as a delivery captain—delivering yachts all over Europe. Mike planned to enter the 1976 OSTAR with sponsorship from a resort in the Bahamas called the *Third Turtle*, which became the name of the boat. What's more, Mike shared Dick's design philosophy, which Dick sums up with the acronym KISS, as in *"keep it simple, stupid."* Jim Brown (Sail Magazine, May 1977) writes, *"Birch commissioned The Third Turtle for the 1976 OSTAR on the premise that the fastest, safest, most comfortable and most economical way to cross the ocean is by taking with you as little as possible, including a small and simple boat."*

Hamilton Ferris entered one, too. Dick describes Ham as an older gentleman, a good sailor. Dick describes Mike as wiry, not a big guy, but strong, light, and quick—built of titanium. *"I sailed with him on his Val and felt completely superfluous. Rather than tell me what he wanted me to do, it was quicker for him to do it."*

Mike made it to the start, as did Rory and Tom. Others weren't so lucky. In addition to Phil Weld in *Gulf Streamer*, Hamilton Ferris capsized his *Val*. Both men were rescued and both boats had to be abandoned. Ham was sitting in our living room describing what happened. He said, *"My God, I capsized to windward."* He was caught by a squall that came in against the wind and threw him back against the waves—a very unusual occurrence.

Weather was a factor leading up to and throughout the race, including a huge gale. Jim Brown, writing for Sail Magazine (May 1977) writes, *"out of 126 starters, only 73 finished by the July 25 cut-off date."* Eric Tabarly of

France, who had won the 1972 OSTAR on a 42-foot boat, was competing this time on a 73-foot ketch *Pen Duick* VI. Eric was so discouraged after the gale that he started home. Mike Birch was equally discouraged—mentally composing an apology letter to Dick while at the helm—but figured he had to deliver the boat so he might as well keep going. For him, the race was over. *"He was so dispirited by the storm that he gave up and just cruised."* Tabarly decided to turn back and finish the race. Rory too was able to finish, but Tom didn't. Tom had equipment problems and ended up having to wait for a part.

First and second place went as expected to two of France's biggest sailing heroes. According to Latitude 38 (May 2005), Eric Tabarly was first to cross the finish line, followed a day later by Alain Colas aboard his gigantic 276-foot, four-masted schooner Club Mediteranee. Latitude 38 reports that Mike finished 11 hours behind Alain Colas.

Writing for *Sail* Magazine in May of 1977, in the article, "Third Turtle Crosses Finish Line", Jim Brown describes Third Turtle's Newport arrival during the 1976 OSTAR:

> On the morning of June 30, there was a mood of relief at the Information Center in Newport, Rhode Island. For three weeks there had been almost daily reports of gales, gear breakage, abandonments and even sinkings undergone by the fleet of singlehanders. But the first two boats had already arrived, and the rush of public interest in the winners had begun to subside. Dennis Blaise, who managed the center, was on duty and enjoying the sunrise when he noticed a little *Val* trimaran

wandering around in the far end of Newport Harbor.

"*No,*" Blaise muttered to himself, "*I can't believe it,*" and reached for the phone to call Newick.

Pat Newick was out of bed but in the state which Dick calls "*BC*" (Before Coffee). She blearily answered the phone and was asked by Blaise, "*Do you have any Val trimarans on a summer cruise in these waters?*"

Pat replied that she didn't think so, asked Dick, and from the bedroom he sleepily responded the same.

During this pause, Dennis Blaise observed from his second-story window in Newport that there was a crowd assembling on the dock. A committee boat hurriedly put out, and then Blaise saw the *Val* tack, which revealed the racing number 66 painted on her topsides. Someone shouted. "*My God! That little sliver of a boat...I can't believe it.*"

Pat heard this commotion when she returned to the phone, and presently Dennis told her, "*I think a Val has just finished the race. Who is number 66?*"

As Pat shuffled through the phone-side papers for the list, she called excitedly to her husband, "*Dick! Who is number 66? They say they think a Val has just finished. I can't believe it!*"

Dick emerged calmly from the bedroom with a very early morning grin and said, *"That's Mike Birch. I can believe it!"*

The event was big news in France, and Newport was crawling with French reporters. Eric Tabarly had already received his country's Legion of Honor for his 1972 win. He and Alain were interviewed endlessly in Newport and greeted back home with a ticker tape parade. However, Alain's second place win was called into question due to broken halyards that required a port stop for repair. It was reported that six people were aboard to help as he left the harbor, when race rules stipulate that he must leave the harbor on his own. Not wanting to disqualify a hero nor his boat sponsored by Club Med, the Royal Western Yacht Club issued a time penalty which brought him down to fifth place—and put Mike into second.

Further controversy erupted when the size of the big boats sparked a debate over size limits, which eventually resulted in new restrictions for the 1980 OSTAR. "I remember the journalists all marveling at our little boat tied up next to this monster French boat and one young, French reporter saying in a thick French accent, "Theez is ze real winnair."

Third Turtle continued to race, captained by Bill Homewood in the 1980 and the 1984 OSTAR, averaging a day less than Mike's time, but was lost en route from the U.S. to Plymouth for her fourth OSTAR, under a new, inexperienced skipper.

Keeping it Simple

Jim Brown, writing for Sail Magazine (May 1977), reported that Eric Tabarly had invested something like a million dollars in *Pen Duick* VI and that Alain Colas's boat cost closer to two million dollars. Brown writes, "*The boat is an extreme statement in modern yacht design, was built especially for this race, and measures 237 feet long.*" Dick's comment was, "*I figured that's no fun: buying first place. I tried to figure another way to win, but the only way I could see to do it was to simplify and make things very, very light. Not luxurious.*"

Jim Brown highlighted the marked contrast between the million-dollar, custom yachts and the off-the-shelf *Val*. He writes, "*The Third Turtle is a stock, production Val class trimaran measuring 31 feet, and costing $24,000 right off the shelf. Her concept is so extraordinarily simple that she was made race-ready for only $2,000 more! All three boats sailed about the same course, fought the same gales and the same calms, and all finished this 24-day North Atlantic race—to windward—within about the same 24-hour period.*"

Which goes to show that Mike was absolutely the right guy to show her off. Dick calls him and Nigel Irons— almost the only non-French people in the serious multihull racing field in those years—two of the bright spots on the international sailing scene, mostly because of their skill and modesty.

The sales brochure for the *Val*s took an equally modest approach. Jim Brown points out that "*in sharp contrast to* the usual designer's ranting about accommodations," the brochure states: *"Two cabins with simple essentials for a couple who appreciate the potential of an easy hundred-mile weekend range."*

Jim Brown, who had inspected several Newick boats, writes that the interiors are just as inventive as the exteriors, *"For what the boats are, their layouts work. The cabins are pleasant and the features have a seamanlike arrangement. Some might say that they are claustrophobic—I would say that they are not spacious."*

By this point in his career, Dick could afford to stand firm on his principles. When asked by Jim Brown if he got a lot of static from his clients for more room, Dick responded, *"There is only one thing we don't have room for and that is compromise."* To illustrate the point, Jim writes that he once overheard Dick talking with a client on the phone, *"The man had apparently called to ask for more room and Newick responded, 'Do you think I'm going to let your wife design my boat for you?'"*

Vals gained in popularity, but only among those who truly appreciated Dick's motto, KISS — keep it simple, stupid. They adapted to the not-spacious interiors. Jim Brown observes, *"They seem willfully to develop an efficient sailing lifestyle to agree with their efficient sailing boats."* Dick didn't concern himself with those who didn't share his philosophy. He ignored their jokes—calling *Vals* transatlantic day sailors because of the lack of amenities—and focused instead on the notion of self-sufficiency, which involved learning to do without modern conveniences—which he always referred to as *inconveniences.* He told Jim Brown: *"The contemporary yachtsman's appetite for fuel, electricity, modern inconveniences and traditional opulence on board must move toward a different kind of self-sufficiency. Less conspicuous consumption and more environmental discipline are now indicated. Dwindling resources and escalating costs already express the need for more efficient boats, and more sailors who appreciate that efficiency."*

Dick's attitude may very well appeal to today's environmentally conscious consumer, but he was ahead of his time. In 1976, the French concept of bigger is better continued to appeal to the public and, most importantly, the sponsors. In the end, it was a battle that Dick couldn't win.

Writing for *Sail* Magazine in May of 1977, Jim Brown beautifully describes the experience of cruising aboard Third Turtle in the article, "Third Turtle Cruises the Cape":

> I was surprised at the stiffness of Turtle. She has extremely wide beam for a multihull her size - 25 feet for a 31 foot trimaran. Thus her stand-up stability is almost flat even when she is close-hauled. Besides standing straight when climbing, she certainly is surefooted. We riders had the sensation that this creature has a gait which does not let it stumble through the water.
>
> The day was gray. The water looked like tarnished pewter, but the sun shone through in shafts to polish it in places. With his usual supercool, Newick directed his creature off the wind. At once we were

joined by the sound of two rushing sluices, one in each of Turtle's tunnels. Our speed had smoothly doubled as we bore away, our motion cut in half and the wind appeared to die completely.

The water simply did not answer; it yielded. It divided itself and ran between the hulls in two brimful flumes. Broad reaching we picked up still more speed. We became obliquely synchronized with the wave train so the boat never really encountered a crest.

Outer vineyard Haven Harbor is a wide bight with high headlands on both points. Something happens to the brisk afternoon southwesterly to cause puffs. It must be that the wind comes curling around the corner, and jumps to fill a local thermo siphon low. As we kept reaching toward the head of the bight, so did the gusts. Turtle responded with pure acceleration: no squatting, no rooting, and no lying down to take it, just more movement straight ahead.

The spray was all below us now, peeling out instead of up, and the "dolphin stays" (those transverse wires underneath the wings) were slicing through this spray and turning it to steam.

We could hear the sounds of all this: the tight wire dolphin stays slicing through torn up water, the vibrating rudder and centerboard giving out their moaning tones, the loud, flat whispers in the wake, and the wind *wooing* as it bent around the sails.

Native and Creative

The innovative wing aka idea of the *Val* Series was used again to launch another successful design, the 38-foot *Native* Class. "Natives were fast cruising boats that could win races."

A total of 15 were built, some of wood, some of foam core fiberglass. Several of the earlier ones were built by Damian McLaughlin of North Falmouth, MA, beginning in 1977.

Jack Petith was among those who successfully raced a *Native*. "*He's a good seaman and it helps that he speaks good French.*" He placed fifth in the first Route du Rhum and first in class in the 1984 OSTAR at the time when the boat was his full time residence.

As of this book's printing, there are two *Native* owners—John Scholberg/Fran Slingerland and Jack Petith—currently more than half way around the world. "*My boats are famous for not having much in the way of accommodation. I figure if you have a dry place to sleep that doesn't jump around under you too much, a place you can stand up and cook, a toilet, and modest storage spaces, you've got the essentials and that will take you around the world.*"

Native

Creative

Just as the *Val* Series inspired the *Native* Series, *Native* inspired the 42-foot *Creative*, a pretty racer/cruiser. *"They could comfortably cruise four people or six, if you had to. She was fast and handy—just a good boat."*

There were only seven built, all of triple diagonal veneer, plywood, epoxy and fiberglass, several in France and one in Canada. The first *Creatives* were built in 1981 by the Lejeloux brothers in La Trinite sur Mer, France.

Creative

Two of the first Creative owners were, Bernard Letellier, a French physician, and Jean Paul Grizeaux, a French attorney and CPA. Jean Paul and Gerard Pesty placed twelfth in the 1981 two person transatlantic race. Another Creative sailed by Yves le Cornec placed 14th in the 1984 OSTAR.

Moxie

The 1976 OSTAR multihulls were becoming important competitors. The 1980 OSTAR was the year they won, and Dick reached what some would say was the pinnacle of his career, with four of his boats competing.

Two of the entries were proas, modeled after *Cheers*. Rory Nugent had originally planned to do the OSTAR in a *Val*, but ended up building two proas. He teamed up with an Englishman named Nick Clifton, who had sailed alone around the world and had sailed a Kelsall trimaran in the 1976 OSTAR. Together, they worked from Dick's line drawing, rather than detailed sketches in order to stay within the budget. They built Rory's 32-foot proa, Godiva Chocolatier (named for the corporate sponsor) and a 42-foot proa Fleury Michon—a great improvement over Cheers, in Dick's estimation—that Nick Clifton planned to race.

There was one further improvement that Dick had suggested, which Clifton thought was unnecessary. Dick recommended adding a quick sheet release to reduce capsize risk.

"Pitch poling can occur when you are steering down a big wave in bad weather—say 15 to 20 foot waves, sailing down the face. The bow is down and the second wave comes quickly and pushes you end over end." The OSTAR is a windward race, so pitch poling isn't an issue. But, getting the boat to the starting line is another story. *"With Cheers, we had a problem. The boat was stable with wind coming from the intended side, less stable when coming*

118

from the other side. So, it behooves the skipper to keep the boat on the right side." That, of course, was Clifton's plan, which worked well until sailed among some logs dropped by a cargo vessel. He hit one and was headed straight for another, so he pulled so hard on the tiller that it came out by the roots, leaving him with no control. *"When he hit the second log, the boat turned the 'wrong' way. The wind was coming from the wrong direction and the boat capsized, which might have been prevented with the simple sheet release that Ian Major had devised for Cheers twelve years earlier."*

Being close to shipping lanes, Clifton was rescued promptly. Rory was not so lucky. His boat capsized in the middle of the Atlantic enroute to the race. Rory sent out an SOS on his Epirb with little hope of being heard, as he was nowhere near shipping lanes. The signal was picked up, however, by an American flyer out on a training mission, who realized after he had returned to base that he very well may have been the only ears out there. He headed out the next day to search and found Rory, who'd been adrift for five days. After his rescue, Rory went on to become an explorer, and very successful writer. His proa was eventually picked up by a Russian vessel. It took 25 years before the current owners, Anne and Paul Buttin, restored her in 2012 and renamed her Lady Godiva.

An even faster Newick design entered in the 1980 OSTAR was Tom Grossman's 56-foot *Kriter VII*, which was hit by a competitor before the start and required 18 hours of repairs before starting the race a day late. Tom persisted and finished 10th.

Also racing in the 1980 OSTAR was Mike Birch on a 46-foot sister ship of *Three Cheers*, named *Olympus* after the photography company sponsor. Mike and Damian McLaughlin built the boat in Damian's shop. Mike finished fourth. If he hadn't had to stop for a repair, Dick thinks he might have won. Instead the honor went to Phil Weld, who won in Newick's 50-footer named *Moxie*. Dick fondly remembers that when Mike Birch came across the line, he held up a sign on a piece of plywood: *"Phil Weld for President."*

Moxie (*photo courtesy of Barbara Bedell*)

Phil Weld

After Phil's *Rogue Wave* was disqualified prior to the 1980 OSTAR, due to size restrictions, Phil was determined to have Dick design a new boat specifically for the race. *Moxie* was built by Walter Green in Falmouth, Maine. *"It was a good boat, but not as "yachty" as Rogue Wave."*

In the winter of 1979, Phil took *Moxie* to the Bahamas to train for the race and reported back to Dick (who had the use of *Rogue Wave* during Phil's absence) that he felt uncomfortable, especially after the rig came down. Phil described in his book, *Moxie*: *"A shroud tang, a tongue-shaped piece of stainless steel joining the backstay to the mast, had broken. I looked out the cabin window just as the mast gently descended into the water."* Dick told him *you've got to realize this is not a small Rogue Wave, it's a big Val."* Phil agreed, and he decided to cut four feet off the mast to make the boat feel safer, especially because at age 65 he was beginning to see himself as an older, perhaps less agile, competitor. It was Phil's age, in fact, that inspired the boat's name. One of Phil's crew on Rogue Wave, enroute to an earlier race, the Route de Rhum—whose medical history included a heart bypass and a pacemaker—joked that he might be in better shape than Phil. It was decided that it takes a lot of *"moxie"* to compete at their age, and the word stuck in Phil's memory, and became the one he painted on the hull of their next creation.

In the 1970s, the word moxie not only brought to mind courage and determination, it brought to mind a drink. Moxie was a beverage company that was known for a carbonated drink, before Coca Cola became the beverage of choice. To avoid possible copyright infringement, Phil wrote to the company to say, *"I hope it's okay with you people that I'm going to name my boat Moxie and it'll give you some great publicity."* But not being a French company, they didn't have a clue, remembers Dick.

Phil, the oldest entrant, won the race in just 18 days, a new record. The press coverage was extensive, with some saying that *Moxie* did more than sail across the Atlantic, she seemed to fly across. American Yacht Review reporter Steve Callahan ("Bird" 1999) wrote that *Moxie* sometimes even outpaced the wind and waves and that Phil Weld *"came to consider the Atlantic his Walden Pond."* After Phil won the race, the company sent him a case of Moxie. *"If it had been a French company, Phil would have been given a parade and a big check."*

Dick loved to tell the story of Phil getting a case of moxie for his win. It provided the perfect counterpoint to the French dominance and growing commercialism of racing. Not only was Dick reluctant to follow the lead to bigger, more expensive boats, he rejected the idea of building corporate sales tools. *"At that time, sponsorship was becoming more important to winning a race, and I was not interested in building and designing sales tools for big corporations. I was simply interested in building good boats for good seamen and women."*

Greed for Speed

Leading up to the 1980 OSTAR, Dick was invited to be part of a multihull mini-symposium event at a technical college in Plymouth, England. His disdain for commercialism—what he dubbed the idea of greed for speed—became the theme of his speech.

By selling out to corporate sponsors, he told the audience, we're moving in a direction with our wonderfully fast multihulls that will come back to bite us in the tail someday. We're winning races at the expense of innovation, of creative discovery. *"Because somebody is spending a million dollars on this thing, you can't take chances, you can't innovate. The business wants to be reasonably sure that it's not taking chances."*

He had hoped to preserve the passion and creativity of the earlier days. No takers. *"They figured Newick didn't have the fire in the belly, what it takes to win a major race."* From that point forward, sponsored boats eclipsed Dick's small boats. Even though Dick's boats continued to win in various classes, his boats didn't get the top prizes, which was all that mattered in some circles.

Looking back, Dick admits he pulled the rug out from under himself, but he says he has no regrets. *"I'm not happy being part of a committee trying to sell somebody's soap. It's not fun."*

Like Phil, Dick was beginning to realize that his age was a factor. *"I could see it coming and maybe I subconsciously realized that I was over the hill in terms of technical ability."* The design industry was becoming more and more specialized. Dick says it harder for one man to design a major boat on his own. You needed materials specialists, rig specialists, coating specialists, and adhesive specialists.

Dick's ideas and environmental concerns didn't resonate at the time. So, even as Dick had been approaching the height of his career, the speech had a negative effect: *"I never got an order from anyone who was serious about winning a race again."*

Moxie: The Retirement Years

After the historic win, Phil had to decide which to keep: *Rogue Wave* or *Moxie*. He decided to give *Moxie* to the Naval Academy. There was a ceremony to thank Phil for his generous gift, which Dick and Pat attended with him.

Phil had hoped the gift would serve to acquaint a whole new generation of sailors with multihulls. But, the idea didn't pan out. Dick says that the acquisition committee chairman wrote into the contract that the boat could never leave the Chesapeake Bay with a midshipman on board. *"Reading between the lines, he was saying everybody knows that multihulls are unsafe. That wording undermined Phil's goal of using the boat to teach midshipmen. And that's the other time I saw Phil lose his cool."*

When the Navy was ready to retire the boat, Dick acted as broker and found the Butlers, the Churchills, and the

Jacobs, friends on Martha's Vineyard to buy her for $90,000. *"The boat had cost a quarter million to build. The three couples had Moxie for many years and anytime they weren't using her, I could. They included me in their sailing parties and I earned my keep by helping to keep things up to snuff. It was a good arrangement for everyone, especially Dick Newick: I had a fine yacht at my disposal on Martha's Vineyard."*

The boat sold again to Jim Rubenstein who, over many years, had Walter Green further improve her. She is now owned by a French marine biologist, who as of this printing, is chartering her in the Mediterranean.

When Phil Weld died, his nautical collection was donated by his wife Ann, at Dick's suggestion, to the Yachting Museum in Newport, Rhode Island. Ann had given Phil's superb sextant to Dick, who felt that it should be shared but not necessarily as part of a museum collection. *"I proposed to the New England Multihull Association that it be used as a perpetual trophy for one of their major races—given to the person voted to have shown the most moxie. I'm pleased that it's still happening."*

Ocean Surfer

While Dick claims that he never got a commission from a serious racer again, following *Moxie's* 1980 OSTAR win, some would argue otherwise. Multihulls Magazine Founder/Editor Charles Chiodi ("A Tribute to A Great Designer: Happy 80th Birthday, Dick Newick!" May/June

2006), for example, believes that Newick's popularity reached its peak in 1980 when *Moxie* won the OSTAR. Charles writes, *"He was one of the most sought-after multihull designers for more than a decade."*

During this period, Dick continued to work on new ideas for subsequent races. But, it wasn't until he was sketching a design for a 40-foot trimaran, speculating ahead to the 1988 OSTAR, that friends, Sue and Alan Butler peeked over his shoulder. Alan was successful in real estate, but described himself as a frustrated architect. He visited Dick occasionally and liked to discuss the drawings. Dick was in the middle of designing a 53 foot trimaran for the Butlers when sketches of the 40 foot *Ocean Surfer* caught Alan's eye.

Dick explained that it was a spec design for the 1988 OSTAR, and had not yet sold. The Butlers thought if nobody else was going to build *Ocean Surfer*, then they'd better. The search for a skipper began. Of course, the famous skippers—mostly from France and some from England—were all taken. Most of the skippers were now in the business of marketing themselves to corporations. They found the sponsor and then they found the designer and builder. The skipper—backed by somebody's soap, as Dick would say—drove the process.

In *Ocean Surfer's* case, the process was less commercial. Designer and owners found the skipper, Mark Rudiger of California, not yet famous on the international scene, and even a modest sponsorship from Holstein Beer in Germany.

Ocean Surfer

The team had their first inkling that Dick may have another winner on his hands when they headed to Florida to test *Ocean Surfer*. During his 500 mile qualifying sail in Florida, Mark was stopped by the Coast Guard on a dark and stormy night about 50 miles off Jupiter, when they had mistaken *Ocean Surfer* for a fast-moving drug boat. *"They figured anybody out there in that terrible weather must have been out there for no good reason."*

"Identify yourself!" came the voice over the radio. Mark did, but the Coast Guard wasn't convinced. *"Heave to. We're coming aboard!"* *"I wouldn't advise that,"* Mark politely replied. He suggested that they come aboard in port instead, but the Coast Guard insisted. Mark was told to stay where he was. He dropped his sail as instructed.

The Coast guard sent a whaleboat. Mark knew the heavy boat would have destroyed *Ocean Surfer* by trying to come along side in those seas. He had a wing mast which gave him maybe six knots if you tweaked it in the right direction. So, every time the whaleboat came close, he'd tweak it. They said, *"Stay where you are; we're coming back with an inflatable. They launched it and promptly capsized. Now wiser, they said, See you in Jupiter in the morning."*

Mark finished second in his class, 14th overall. Dick lamented that the boat ended up too heavy. *"My fault. But she'd often do over 20 knots with minimal effort."*

One of the boat's principal features was that the mast could be raked to windward to make it more efficient. This was achieved by placing the foot of the mast on a track. In conditions where it was useful, the skipper could rake the mast eight or ten degrees and get up to two more knots. Dick says the French started about that time to rake the masts on their 60-foot trimarans, but they did it by keeping the mast centered and having hydraulic adjusters on the shroud—expensive, but it also worked.

After the race, the Butler's converted *Ocean Surfer* to a cruiser, which gave them many years of good service.

Dick designed another racer named *Val II* for the 2000 OSTAR (which by then had been named the Europe One Star) but found no takers. He wrote about the experience as part of an article for Multihulls Magazine's 25th Anniversary Issue (Jan/Feb 2000.) Dick wrote, *"Racing with a minimum of rules can show what works best at sea, especially with only one or two in the crew, but when pressure to win dominates, informal fun is diluted, at least for me. So, I am not involved in serious sponsored racing these days, preferring to concentrate on simpler cruising boats, fast enough to do well in an occasional race. However, when a friend suggested that I should have a boat in the 2000 OSTAR I couldn't resist sketching a 30-footer which would have been the smallest boat in the race (that way we could surely brag that we weren't beaten by a larger boat, and could take some pleasure from all those we did beat.) She would be uncomfortable for one to live aboard for 15 to 20 days, but would be a good daysailer after the race. Rig and connecting structure would be much like Ocean Surfer, a 1988 racer. She could be made very light with modern, no longer exotic, materials. Simply outfitted: priced accordingly. We didn't find the right client, but there will be other races."* Four have been built, but not yet raced.

PART THREE

Moving to Maine

When Dick heard that Jackie Onassis had bought 300 acres on the Martha's Vineyard, he joked, *"Well, there goes the neighborhood!"* The Vineyard had become crowded with tourists, just as had happened on St. Croix.

The Newicks weren't ready to retire, and Dick never would be, but they were ready for a change. *"We wanted to move not so much with retirement in mind but with slowing down, doing more of what we wanted to do. The kids were grown. We had freedom that we didn't have earlier."* Also, they wanted to live in what Dick calls the real world, where people grew things and made things. That place became Maine.

With slowing down in mind, Dick had been working each summer while on Martha's Vineyard on a 51-foot trimaran cruiser that he and Pat could live aboard. *"We could only work over summer months because epoxy needs heat to cure."*

As a joke, the building crew, mostly vacationing students, wrote, "Pat's" on the bow. Pat said, *"Who are you kidding? This is Dick's boat."* But the name stuck, even years later after it had been sold to a Swiss attorney.

It took ten summers to complete *Pat's*. When she was finally ready to launch, Dick realized *"She was intended for us to live aboard for months at a time. But, she was designed ten years before we launched her. Our situation was different back then. Pat would not choose to live on a boat full time—having to put ice aboard every two to three days, taking laundry ashore. All the little inconveniences are often in her lap, not in mine. So, it didn't work."*

Pat's

Pat had summed up her feelings about long term sailing when the four Newicks cruised on *Ay Ay* with the Morris family. They sailed from St. Croix down to Grenada, island hopping along the way. On one particularly rough passage with waves of 20-30 ft., Pat had found shelter from the wind and spray under Halsted Morris' yellow, inflatable raft. She was amazed to hear Tootie, seemingly enjoying every minute of it, composing limericks. Not to be outdone, Pat sat up long enough to recite her impromptu poem….*"I lay beneath the yellow raft, hoping that our sailing craft, that bounced and pitched in waves so steep, interfering with my sleep, would soon reach land where I could rest, old terra firma suits me best."*

After they left the Vineyard, however, it worked for a summer of exploring Maine. So, Dick sailed the boat up the coast, and Pat drove to meet him there. *"We had been up there looking around for years. My first stop after leaving the Vineyard was Kittery. We hop-scotched up the coast for the whole summer. We knew a lot about all the harbors and back roads of Maine before that summer was over."*

In August, Dick and Pat sailed up the Damariscotta River and spent time with the Weld family who had a summer place on the river. Dick enjoyed piling all the Weld grandchildren on the boat for a sail. *"By this time, Phil had died and Anne was living in a 3,000+ square foot summer place. She went back to her home in Gloucester, MA for the winter, and offered it to us until spring."* So, the Newicks continued to explore Maine by car, with the luxury of a riverfront home base. It was expensive to heat, according to Dick, but it was a rare opportunity to live in such style.

"I told Pat we're never going to live in a place where we could have a hundred of our closest friends for lunch. Let's invite everyone in the boat business to Maine for a social day. We see all these people at boat shows, but only for brief conversations."

Ninety-five people came. There was no agenda, save for a single guest speaker: John Letcher, a hull design software pioneer. *"He was a brilliant guy. I bought his software which was very expensive and took a course from him, back when I was trying to learn computer design."*

"We eventually bought a piece of land in Kittery Pt., on the edge of a salt marsh, which was part of a Rachel Carson Wildlife Sanctuary. The main 'wildlife' was mosquitoes, but the stream was a great place to kayak, and fun for our six grandchildren to come for visits."

While Dick was in the process of slowing life down, work came in enough to keep him busy. *"I had a wait list of people interested in designs."* Most of my clients were happy; the only unhappiness was when I was late."

Echo

About the time that the Newicks moved to Maine, Dick started work on the new *Echo* class. The 36-foot trimaran was designed at the instigation of Max Purnell, Dick's New Zealand agent. Actually, Dick's only agent anywhere.

When I was becoming known in the design business, I'd get letters from all over the world saying, *"I want to be your agent"*. I'd say, *"Well, that would be interesting. First thing you have to do is buy a set of plans and build a boat so you know what you are selling."* They usually evaporated quickly. Max, a native of New Zealand, managed a dairy farm on St. Croix where they met and became friends. It was Dick who approached Max about becoming an agent. *"On his way home to New Zealand, he and his wife, Maggie, stopped on the Vineyard and bought plans for the 36-foot, Tricia. He later sold a dozen sets of plans in New Zealand."*

Max raced his *Tricia*, around New Zealand and did well. Twelve years after buying the plans he wanted to know what Dick had in mind for improvements. Dick, in fact, had been thinking along those lines. Max suggested a round bottom version—an echo of *Tricia*. The first of several was launched in 1994 for a 747 pilot who flew for the national Chinese airlines. His boat was built in the

Philippines and raced in Thailand where he won the region's most prestigious race, the King's Cup, three times. In all, about a dozen Echoes were built, and an Echo II stock design added.

Echo

Dick's presence in New Zealand prompted an article by Australian writer Philip Thomson, which was published by Multihulls Magazine in 1997. In it, Phil tours the island, meeting Max Purnell and visiting with various *Echo, Tremolino, Val and Val II* builders and sailors. Phil writes, *"I saw the special float shape that Dick Newick invented, called a New Moon Ama. In curving the outside of the float in the direction opposite to the normal tumblehome, Newick gets some dynamic lift when the boat moves. The boats have canted centerboards in the floats to help lift the float and improve handling at speed."*

Later, Dick discussed the New Moon Ama in an article he wrote for Multihulls Magazine's 25th Anniversary Issue (Jan/Feb 2000). He wrote, *"Multihull stability depends on two things: weight and overall beam. As boats get lighter they must get wider to carry a given sail area. Only exceptions are to add 'daggerfoils' in the amas, or have 'new moon' amas for dynamic stability. Also, the rig can be inclined to windward to decrease heeling moment."*

Phil goes on to describe *"another Newick idea"* which is to *"design the centerboard case for collision with things, by using a crash box. Basically, the bottom of the case is made longer than needed by about 200 mm. A piece of high-density foam is shaped to fit both the back of the case and the board, so that when the board hits something, the foam crushes and the top forward edge of the board moves against a big fiberglass spring. When Max hit a rock in the Coastal Classic, he only had to remove remnants of the old foam and replace it before continuing. It seems a little more sensible in some ways than having sacrificial tips to the centerboards as we have done with our catamaran."*

Phil next visits Murray and Lloyd *"partners in another Echo just up the road"* which they were building for cruising, not racing. *"It was interesting to see this tri being built as a cruiser. It seems that the breed is suffering a little in Australia but in New Zealand modern bridge-deck cats seem to be the uncommon breed and tris are still seen as valid cruisers."*

Phil goes to Auckland to see an *Echo* being built by Tony Lawson, then on to see Hamish Russell's nearly completed *Echo*. *"Hamish has Newick trimarans in the genes. Not only did he build the main hull of Murray and Lloyd's boat, but both his brothers have built, or are building Newicks."*

Phil observes, *"Newick's boats are also different from other modern multis in that he still likes the structural characteristics of wood over glass. There is a largish wooden keel in the boat and wooden reinforcing around the centerboard case and bulkheads. Max Purnell said that Newick likes the fatigue resistance and toughness of wood saying that in resistance to fatigue it was second only to carbon fiber."*

Bird

Even as his designs found their way to buyers around the world, Dick's ideas continued to evolve, with great results when matched with the right owner and builder. A case in point is *Bird*, one of the 48-foot Traveler Class designs, built for Andy and Joyce Green of Port Arthur, Texas and built by Lone Star Multihulls in Brownsville. Andy was looking for ease of sailing and maintenance; comfort at sea, and, above all, speed. Newick delivered.

Bird made headlines in 1999 when a story by Steve Callahan appeared in American Yacht Review.   In it, Newick compared *Bird* to *Moxie*, saying that Weld's *Moxie* was state-of-the-art at the time, and that Green's *Bird* is comparable.

In the article, Andy says, "*I'd run companies with lots of people, and I didn't want to need a medium-sized navy to run a boat. It looked like a multihull would offer us more speed with fewer crew.*"

Andy had owned a Santa Cruz 50 ULDB, but was drawn to multihulls after seeing how even moderate ones like the Condor 40 could outpace the monohull racers. He tried a Condor and enjoyed it four years before starting *Bird*. Dick had originally drawn the *Traveler* for another client, who ended up having to table the project. A long-time Newick fan, Andy saw the plans and, according to Steve, thought it reflected Newick's best and newest thinking. He took over the project, which was originally designed for wood-epoxy construction.   He reengineered it.   Steve writes, "*A structural and materials engineer, Green had worked for General Dynamics and on such projects as the breakthrough, composite-bodied Formula 1 racer Chaparral. He founded Composite Technology, Inc. and had been involved with building Olympic Solings and Flying Dutchmans as well as larger race boats.   Green reengineered Newick's design for composite construction, working closely with Newick and Lone Star. Lone Star had previously built a number of Chris White multihulls, but this was the first time they used ATC Core-Cell, a strip planked foam core. Newick now says the system is his favorite way to build a one-off boat."* Lone Star agreed.

Bird (drawing by Bruce Alderson)

Bird was roomier than most Newick designs. It had to be, because the Greens wanted both a racer and a cruiser. Though passionate about racing, Andy's wife, Joyce, often joins him for the 600 to 800 mile cruise home. The result deviates from what Steve calls the trademark Newick look: banana sheer lines, the ski-slope front to the cabin top leading to a low-slung foredeck, and freeboard close to the water. It's a compromise that Dick has done before. Dick, who sometimes refused to compromise his design philosophy, has grown over time to be more accommodating. According to Steve, Dick designed a reverse-sheer 50-footer back in 1980 for racing, and a newer, small trimaran design called Wings in the 90s, both to meet the client's needs. By adding a little extra surface area and weight, the client gains space inside the hulls. In the article, a mellower Dick says, *"The amas (outer hulls) are so big, I'd be happy cruising and camping out in them."*

In his 1999 article for *American Yacht Review* entitled "Pulling out the Stops", Steve Callahan described how Andy Green pulls out the stops when racing versus cruising:

In the heavier airs, she'll certainly need no help. Green has revved her up to 24 knots in winds blowing 18 to 25 (30 to 35 apparent), and that's with plain sail. He'll soon carry two spinnakers, the largest almost 2,000 square feet, almost double her working sail. To further ease handling, the jib could be made self-tacking, as the one Green now carries barely laps the mast. The boat is certainly mainsail driven. For deliveries and cruising, Green carries a simple triangular main with no battens, which his wife loves.

For racing, he pulls out the stops and raises a carbon-battened, full-roach Kevlar powerhouse. The sails hang on a common aluminum mast—double diamonds of rod rigging keep the stick in column while half-inch Dieform forestay and two shrouds hold it upright—the shrouds significantly swept back, which is possible because the boat's immense beam keeps them out of the way of the mainsail even when it's eased.

Steve Callahan continues: that even in 20-plus knots of wind with full sail, *Bird* has never flown the main hull. *"Her hulls have a lot more rocker to their bottoms and their ends are more V'd, providing a softer motion in a seaway. In addition, Newick thinks the volume of the amas is often excessive these days, and that the 140% of designed displacement that Bird can carry is more than enough."*

White Wings

Flying Fish

Tremolino

Limmershin (Tom Robbins)

Bayou Belle

Vaka Fanaua
designed by Dick Newick

THE LAST DESIGN, 'VAKA FANAUA'

Dick and Pat started their lives together in the Caribbean in 1957, and discovered their second love, New Zealand in 1997. Their daughter, Val and her husband, Richard Wright, had residency permits and lived up on the Northland near Whangaroa Harbor. It was there that Dick first saw the beautiful, sleek, Maori canoes, and couldn't resist sketching them, but with sails, of course.

When Dick gave a copy of his drawings to his friend, Max Purnell, they became the seed that germinated into a whole new plan ... a cargo boat for the islands of Tonga. Max's brother-in-law, Sitiveni Halapua, was a distinguished member of the Tongan Parliament, and he quickly recognized that the Maori canoe drawings might inspire

146

Dick to design a power/sail cargo boat. A replacement was desperately needed for the previous steel cargo vessel that sank with many lives lost. Sitiveni and his wife, Janet, hired Dick to do some sketches they could present to the Tongan community for their approval.

(*Photo by Ezra Newick*)

The Tongan people decided to do their own fund raising and to become the sole owners of the cargo boat. Construction began in 2013 at Aaron Beattie's boatyard, Lifestyle Yachts in Pipiroa, New Zealand.

(*Photo by Ezra Newick*)

In a 2011 NEMA (New England Multihull Association) article, Phil and Amy Babcock, quote Dick: "*VAKA FANAUA (meaning 'two-masted sailing vessel' in the Tongan language) combines old Pacific Island tradition with modern construction to safely and quickly carry almost three tons of people and/or cargo on deep sea voyages.*

"*She can average about 10 knots in usual trade wind conditions, which conveniently blow from the east. A small diesel engine will give an economical 6 to 8 knots in a calm and increase her maneuverability in small, shallow harbors closed to larger vessels. A 14 foot tender is carried to load and deliver people and goods to islands without a harbor.*

"Wood construction sheathed with epoxy and fiberglass gives a moderate first cost, and, equally important, low maintenance so the boat is affordable to operate by islanders."

Afterward

In 2000, Dick was invited by the publishers of Multihulls Magazine to write an article about his career for the magazine's 25th Anniversary issue (Jan/Feb 2000). In the article, Dick reflected on what he considers multihulls' real roots—not the rock-star racers of the Atlantic but the early settlers of the Pacific. In fact, he takes little credit for his contributions to the sport, believing instead that he is simply rediscovering what an ancient culture surely knew: *"This is MULTIHULLs 25th year in publishing, my 43rd year enjoying all kinds of multihulls. Multiply either of those numbers by 100 and that's how long ago the Southeast Asians had already started to explore and settle the islands of the Pacific Ocean, one fifth of the world's surface—in multihulls. Re-learning what they knew has been a fascinating experience."*

Dick expects that this fascinating knowledge—will be useful to the next generation of designers. And, while he's certainly made his mark in the world of racing, he hopes that his achievements will have a more far-reaching effect. In fact, the impact he most hopes to make is not on racing, but on the environment. An environmentalist long before the term was in vogue, Dick's designs have always pointed to a simpler way of life. He's bothered by excess. From the mega yachts that now dominate racing to the fuel guzzling fishing boats that supply today's markets, Dick sees a planet in peril. In his greed for speed speech, Dick pointed out that *"the world's fishermen now burn a kilo of fuel to catch a kilo of fish, an unacceptable ratio which challenges us to develop better ways to use the wind."*

A traditional Vallom

In his experience with the Seri Indians in the 1950's and another in the 1990's with the fishermen of Kerala, India, Dick tried and failed to convince them to make at least some use of wind power. He'd been invited by the Catholic Church Society in Alleppey to visit the region with Spencer Apollonio from Maine, to hopefully find ways to help the local fishermen improve their boats.

Russell Long from San Francisco, California heard about the plan and offered to help—an offer gratefully accepted by the Society members and Dick, but the offer had a proviso. Everyone involved would need to agree on using a plan called, *"The Participatory Method."* That meant that Church Society members, the fishermen, boat shop workers, Dick, Pat, Russell, all had equal voices in any decisions to be made. It was a revolutionary concept and it was hoped the project would become a means of empowerment for local people who were conditioned within the hierarchical structure to have few, if any choices.

Dick, Russell and the shop crew

Russell Long wrote his Harvard PHD thesis on the Participatory Method, describing how those months in Southern India rewarded, but tested those involved in the project. It was especially frustrating for Dick during meetings with the fishermen's committee, having to patiently wait for the members to decide if they would accept his suggestions. He designed and made a model of a sailing proa, which they eventually approved of for an 8-

meter (26ft 2+) boat. Dick's suggestion for improving the Valloms' (the local traditional boats) seaworthiness by replacing rope/tar seams with epoxy resin was more readily accepted. It took many weeks setting up a boat shop, making do with whatever tools were available in the small town of Alleppey, and training workers to build the proa and replace the seams of a recently purchased Vallom.

The rebuilt Vallom

On launching day, a reconstructed Vallom and a brand new sailing proa slid into the Arabian Sea with exhausted, but grateful Dick and Russell, proudly helping. In three months, with the help of many local workers plus Dick Illamarino and Andy Bartholomew, the shop was prepared to continue rebuilding Valloms and constructing additional proas.

In the end, the pressures from larger, commercial fishing vessels, capable of reaching the same fishing grounds faster, forced the fishers to abandon the proa. They needed their bigger and bigger motors to be competitive. This double-edged sword was causing a rapid depletion of fish, not only in the Arabian Sea, but all around the world.

Launching day

Reconstructing Valloms was somewhat successful, but acquiring enough epoxy resin would be an ongoing problem. More than that, however, was a cultural divide among an established hierarchy that prevented the fishermen and boat shop workers from having truly equal voices and ownership of the boats they built.

In the conclusion of Russell Long's thesis, he wrote:

> Success for me involved much more than just the boat's commercial viability. It involved the establishment of a cross-cultural, collaborative dialogue which could become a template for many other small-scale development projects by others in the future. It involved the construction not just of boats, but of honest, non-exploitative relationships, of friendships, and of deep understandings which are forged from jointly confronting difficult social problems. It involved sharing the pains of minor failure and setback, and celebrating the small and large successes where they were found. Ideally, it would lead to a deepening awareness of the myriad social, cultural, and ecologic issues surrounding development in India or other developing countries, and would provide a further tool from which to create positive social change.

Of course, Dick had made a career out of developing better ways to use the wind, which he summed up in the anniversary article—in his modest, no-nonsense style—in one simple sentence: *"I have enjoyed introducing new concepts over the years, including pivoting, variable height outboard motor mounts; unstayed, rotating masts for Ljungstrom rigs in multihulls; daggerfoils, daggerboard safety devices; proas with the ama to leeward; pivoting rudders that swing aft if struck; master pattern hull lofting; wing aka trimarans; and single ama power outriggers."*

These and other innovations were developed to win races. They were subjected to one of the ultimate tests, the OSTAR. It is Dick's hope that they will stand the test of time; that he will be remembered not just for his racing designs, but that his insights might be useful for a greater good. His greed for speed speech began: *"I have been asked to discuss racing multihull design and will do so at the risk of being stereotyped as a racing multihull designer. I would prefer to simply be known as a boat designer."* It ended with a simple wish: *"We hope that our racing experience will be useful."*

In 2004, he was honored by the New England Multihull Association with a lifetime achievement award. Bill Doelger, a close friend, presented the award to Dick with these comments:

> In the history of multihull design, Arthur Piver is generally considered as the father figure of the modern multihull. Dick Newick was almost his contemporary. Where Piver was the brash revolutionary, Dick became the interpretive artist. He brought beauty and elegance to multihull design. A Newick design has a recognizable style that more closely resembles the natural curves of a sea creature, but his designs were not just pretty boats. The history of the Single Handed Trans Atlantic Race is the best demonstration of Dick's success.

At the end of his presentation, Bill said, "*I am particularly honored to make this award because my sailing career began when I went for a ride with Dick on his boat in October of 1974. That ride changed my life.*"

Four years later, he was inducted into the North American Boat Designers Hall of Fame where he joined the ranks of such luminaries as Nat and L. Francis Herreshoff, John Alden, Phil Rhodes, Olin Stephens, Ray Hunt, and Jack Hargraves.

In 2004 Dick and Pat left Maine and took another look at Mexico in their 19-foot motor home before moving to beautiful Sebastopol, California.

Most of his archives now reside in the Mariners' Museum of Newport News, Virginia. Dick is grateful to the good folks at the Mariners' Museum for preserving and documenting multihull development. Thanks to their efforts, future generations will have an opportunity to do the same.

In Dick's 86th year, 2012, he was invited to join Andy Bartholomew, who was sailing on his 50-foot *Traveller* from Auckland, New Zealand, to San Francisco. Andy, at age 75, was planning to sell Traveler for a smaller sailboat. The first leg of his trip was with one crew to Tahiti, and from there he sailed solo to the big island of Hawaii. He and Dick met in Kona.

Traveller (*Photo by Brent Levenson*)

Dick wrote of the trip:

"OLD SAILORS RULE!"

The rig on Andy Bartholomew's 50-foot trimaran, *Traveller*, which I designed many years ago, came down with him and me aboard last month. We were 500 miles north of Hawaii bound for San Francisco at the time, sailing in 15 to 20 knots of wind, with 9-ft. seas. We were carrying a working jib and a double-reefed main. Our boat speed was over nine knots.

The cause of the dismasting was a chainplate toggle that didn't match the turnbuckle. It took a day for us—Andy is 75 and I'm 86—to get the deck squared away, spars secured, and sails stowed. The carbon fiber wing mast was damaged at the leading edge below the hounds.

We got underway with a 185-sq. ft. staysail. We hoisted the foot on the radar mast, which was well aft, and secured the head as far forward as possible to windward. With 15 to 20 knots of wind, which we had all the way to Oahu, we were able to make 1.5 knots.

When we used the engine—which was more than half the time—we ran it at just 2,000 rpm to conserve fuel. We had 50 gallons of fuel and that got us within 130 miles of Oahu. The University of Hawaii research vessel Kilo Moana diverted their course to supply Dick and Andy with enough fuel to reach port the next day.

Dick wrote, *"Andy Bartholomew is a fine seaman and shipmate, which minimized his elderly guest's shortcomings. We were pleased to have been able to make it back to Honolulu with no more assistance needed."*

And in May, 2013, Dick was invited to France for the annual Golden Oldies gathering where he was honored with 11 of his designs assembled in Sete harbor. It was for him, *"the icing on the cake."* He was among many of his French friends who understood, admired, and appreciated his dedication as he did theirs.

Dick Newick died peacefully at home, surrounded by his family, on August 28, 2013.

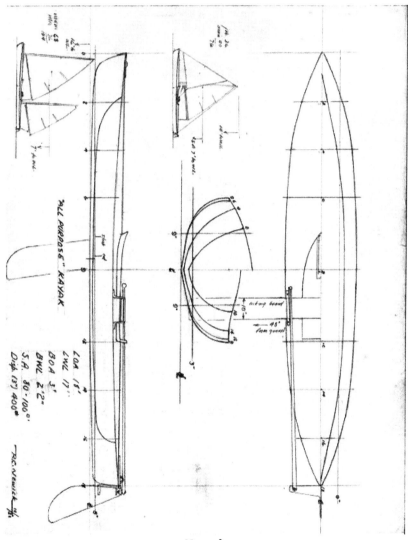

"ALL PURPOSE" KAYAK

LOA 18'
LWL 17'
BOA 3'
BWL 2'2"
S.A. 80-100°
Disp. 137 400#

R.C. NEWICK '76

Kayak

159

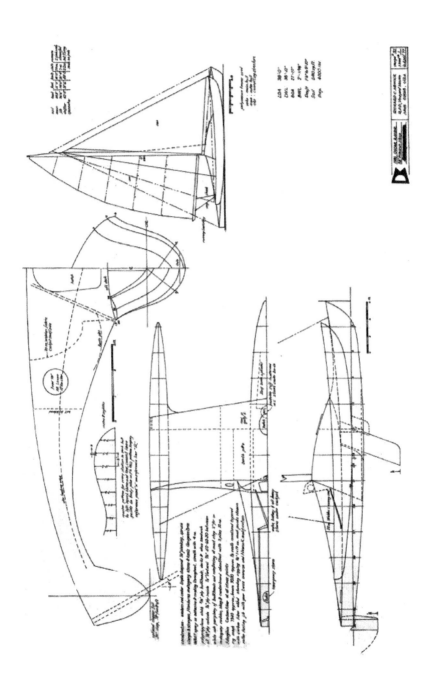

1980 Ostar, proposed drawing, (trimaran sloop)

160

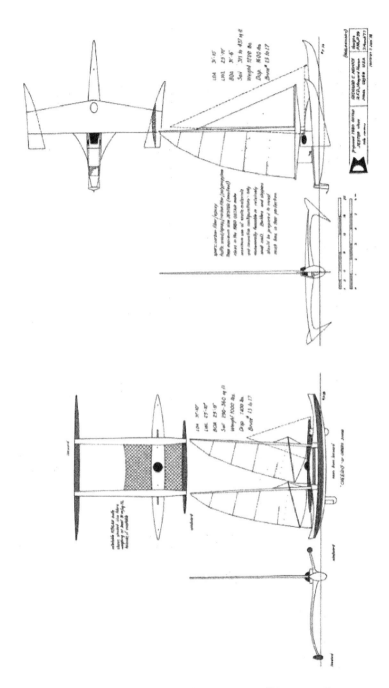

1980 Ostar, proposed drawing, ("Jester")

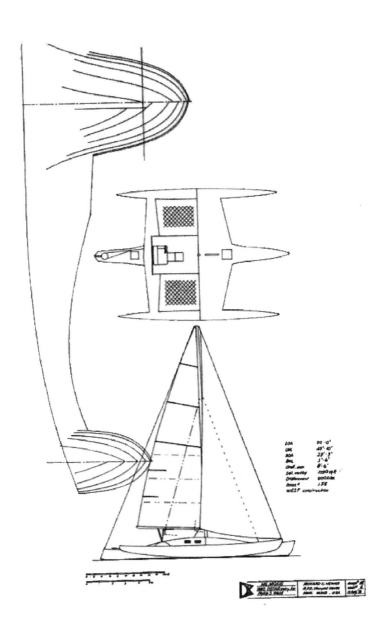

"Moxie"

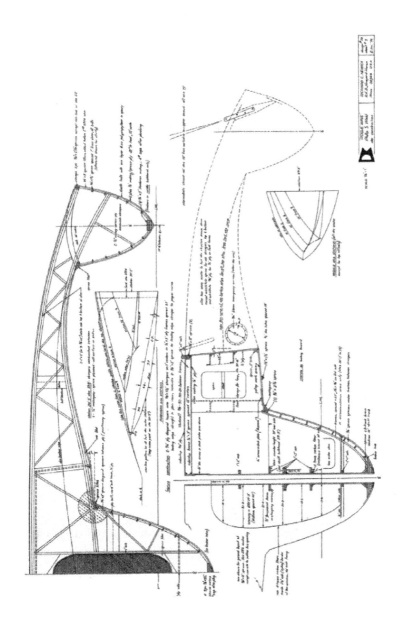

"Rogue Wave"

163

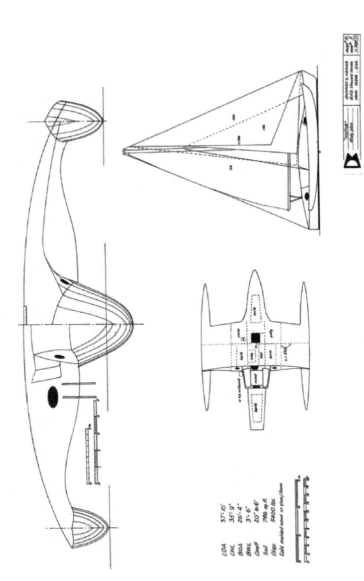

LOA 37'-10"
LWL 35'-9"
BOA 26'-4"
BWL 3'-6"
Draft 20" to 6'
Sail 786 sq ft.
Disp. 5400 lbs.
Cold molded wood or glass/foam

"Native"

164

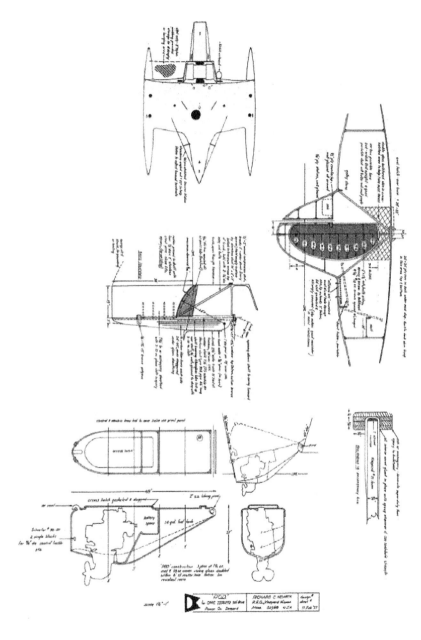

"Pod"

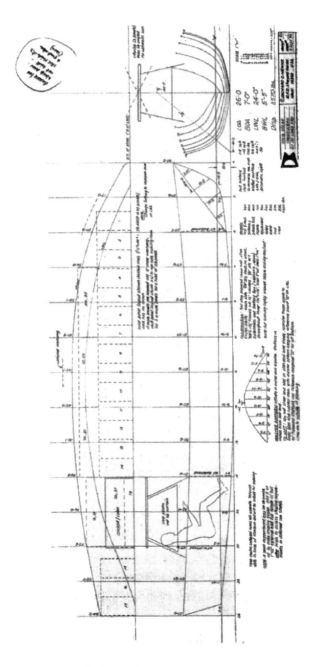

Solo solar trans-ocean

166

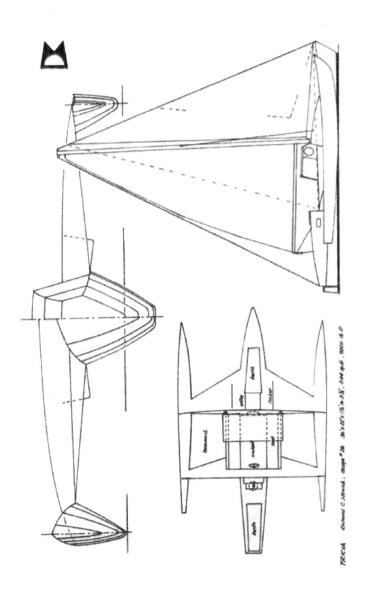

Tricia

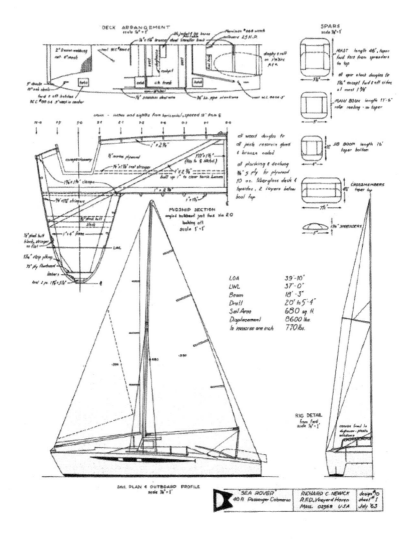

"Sea Rover"

Comments:

Jim Brown (USA)

"What I have always admired is his purity, his confidence in his decisions, and most of all his art, his aesthetic sensibilities and how those three were so integrated in his thinking and his person."

Jack Petith (Thailand)

Thank you Dick for imagining my Native 38, Naga, into reality. Such a great boat. I've just had to keep her and sail her for over 30 years now--my racing house, as I used to call her. A wonderful, beautiful home—always the best looking boat in the anchorage—and a fantastic sailor that has carried me uncounted miles in every condition. Quick and nimble, reliable, predictable, with perfect manners and no big surprises. And fast, of course. Dick's work was genius. Dreams into reality. Thank you Dick. Naga is a living monument to you.

Drs. Cesare Giorgi & Daria Riva (Italy)

"Barbaresco" has been our sailing companion for 32 years, during which we had more than several occasions to thank the designer for her performances, strength, and above all, the ease with which she handled the sea; we used to call her "our sea Cadillac." Dick has been an affectionate friend. He used to call us, "my favorite Italian doctors."

Dr. Bernard Letellier (France)

"Grand Charles" was delivered at the end of 1980. Dick came back very satisfied by the building quality. At the first trial, I remember Dick's glimpse of his new design, enjoying works of the hulls, form of stem wave, light wake, passing over swells, all in suppleness, a huge seagull skimming water. At sea we have simply clinked glasses of bottled cider, made by my father, apple fragrance blended with sea smell, for the long life of Creative. Dick concluded, it's a new step in speed and comfort.

Craig Alexander (France)

I was the owner of Moxie for a few years. I had quite a few moments in my sailing career and have to say I cherish my times with Dick more than most. He was such a soft spoken gentle man with such a vision of design. I once in 1980 had the chance to race in the St. Barths regatta with Phil Weld on Rogue Wave, after the race I told myself one day I would have a boat like that, and along came Moxie, the chance of a lifetime for me.

I will always remember and relay to others when they have ideas for improvement on Dick's designs, they work, do not change them and keep it simple.

Jens Quorning (Denmark)
- designer and builder of Dragonfly Trimarans Denmark

I'm extremely proud and honored that Dick gave me the opportunity and trust to work with him back in 1983-84 on Martha's Vineyard, where I, as a young boat builder learned so much from Dick in design, construction methods and introduced me to the U.S. multihull community. This has ever since been a deep part of me.

After some serious repair work on 'Rogue Wave,' Dick also arranged that I sailed back to Europe on 'Rogue Wave' with Tom Follett as skipper (his last trans-Atlantic crossing) and Rick Haslet, (Dick's cousin) a trip that I beforehand could only dream of.

Dick was really one of the great and biggest pioneers in modern times of multihull design, to believe and work so dedicated with these great boats was so deep in his DNA and he did this with a great, special passion. Dick also cared a lot for the poor third world and did his best to design simple boats to make poor people's lives better. Also, as a person, he had his interesting opinions about life and politics, and of course his special humor we shall never forget.

Dick has been a great inspiration, a true and a close friend, and he will always be close to me!

Acknowledgments:

Alison Cotter: her interviews and manuscript

Liza Blair: granddaughter, editor at large

Ben Blair: grandson, artist

Ezra Newick: grandson, ace photographer

Authors, magazines, and friends ......

Jim Brown: eloquent, humorous Sail magazine articles, photos, lifelong friend

Steve Callahan: whose articles captured the essence of Dick's philosophy

Meade Gougeon: world-renowned epoxy guru, multi-tasking friend

James Munves: author, publisher, advisor

Max Purnell: Long time Kiwi friend, Tongan cargo boat organizer, collaborator

Bruce Alderson: artist of the famous Cheers poster and other Newick designs

Phil Thompson: writes for Multihulls with several about Dick's designs

Russell Long: environmentalist, activist, sailor, documentary film maker

Phil and Amy Babcock—their NEMA article, for helping to introduce Vaka Fanaua to the world....

Jan Classen: special thanks for her photo editing

Ashlyn Brown: advisor

And those no longer here to accept our appreciation….

Les Moore, who realized Dick wouldn't take time to write his own story and arranged for his daughter Alison Cotter to write the manuscript. Very special thanks to Les and Alison.

Fritz Henle for photos

Martin Luray & Jack Knights for their articles

Charles Chiodi: founder of Multihulls magazine

And the publications…

Rudder & Latitude 38

Bibliography

Jim Brown: "No Room for Compromise," Sail Magazine, May 1977

Steve Callahan: "Bird," American Yacht Review, 1999

Charles Chiodi: "A Tribute to A Great Designer: Happy 80th Birthday, Dick Newick!" Multihulls Magazine, May/June 2006.

Bill Doelger: Presentation of Lifetime Achievement Award to Dick Newick, New England Multihull Association, February 7, 2004

L. Francis Herreshoff: Personal Letter to Dick Newick, May 2, 1966

L. Francis Herreshoff: Personal Letter to Dick Newick, July 8, 1960

Jack Knights: Jack Knights Scans the Racing Scene, (Yachts and Yachting), March 27, 1970, p. 763

Latitude 38, May 2005 (no writer listed; great recap of dick's 50 years, writer calls it a "delightful portrait of an old school yacht designer)

Martin Luray: "Dick Newick: Quick Quicker Quickest," Rudder, May 1974

Elizabeth McMullen: "A Bird's Eye View," Yachting World, Nov 1975

Dick Newick: "Greed for Speed," Notes for Speech Delivered at a Symposium just before the 1980 OSTAR

Philip Thompson: "Newicks in New Zealand," Multihulls, September/October 1997, 12-15.

Phil and Amy Babcock: NEMA newsletter Fall 2011

CPSIA information can be obtained at www.ICGtesting.com
Printed in the USA
BVOW06s2054061115

425659BV00009B/127/P